THE GOSPEL ACCORDING TO LEVITICUS

A daily devotional for a neglected book

BRIAN H. EDWARDS

DayOne

© Day One Publications 2024

ISBN 978-1-84625-781-0

British Library Cataloguing in Publication Data available

Scripture quotations in this publication are from the Holy Bible, New International Version (NIV), copyright © 1973, 1978, 1984, 2011, International Bible Society. Used by permission of Hodder and Stoughton, a member of the Hodder Headline Group. All rights reserved.

Published by Day One Publications
Ryelands Road, Leominster, HR6 8NZ
Telephone 01568 613 740
North America Toll Free 888 329 6630
email—sales@dayone.co.uk
web site—www.dayone.co.uk

All rights reserved
No part of this publication may be reproduced, or stored in a retrieval system, or transmitted, in any form or by any means, mechanical, electronic, photocopying, recording or otherwise, without the prior permission of Day One Publications.

Printed by 4edge Limited

Why read Leviticus?

Have you ever read through the book of Leviticus and enjoyed it—or even understood it?

The introduction to one nineteenth century commentary on Leviticus opens with this statement: 'Perhaps no book in the Bible presents to the ordinary reader so many and peculiar difficulties as the book of Leviticus.'[1] If that was true back then, it is certainly true today. Leviticus must head the list of books in the Bible that are least attractive for Christians in the twenty-first century. There is little narrative and yet pages of seemingly tedious and repetitive details of the religious ceremonies of ancient Israel's worship. We know it must be relevant or it would not be in the Bible, but what is its significance for those who live under the New Covenant of Jesus Christ?

To many readers the book may appear mysterious, irrelevant, even ungodlike in its expectations and impractical in its demands. Perhaps it should not be part of Scripture?

There is no doubt that Jesus believed Leviticus was part of the Jewish *Torah*. The command he gave to the healed lepers (Matthew 8:4) was supported only by Leviticus 14:3–10; his particular reference to the shewbread reserved for the priests (Matthew 12:4) is found in Leviticus 24:9 alone; and when he spoke of the renewal of circumcision 'to Moses', the only passage he could have in mind is Leviticus 12:1–3.

However, the cherished but now ageing view of liberal criticism will have none of this. Some still insist, without evidence, that Leviticus, along with the other four books of the Pentateuch, was

---

1 S. H. Kellogg, *The Book of Leviticus* (Hodder and Stoughton, 1891). Even today, one of the best straightforward and accessible commentaries on Leviticus.

invented by Jewish scribes when the Jews returned from their scattered exile in the fifth century BC, sometime around the time of Ezra and Nehemiah; they made up this forgery to provide a 'history' for the Jews. The inevitable conclusion is that when the scribes wrote 'The LORD spoke to Moses'—fifty-six times in this book—they knew it was not true. So successful was the forgery of these deceitful holy men, that no one, Jew or Christian, ever uncovered the deception until the time of the critics in the late nineteenth century AD! Apparently, even Jesus was either equally misled or he deliberately supported what he knew was a fraudulent claim. Either way, he was not who he claimed to be, and we can trust little else that he taught.

However, reading Leviticus, even for those who trust the authority of Jesus, can he hard going. When John Currid worked on his detailed commentary on Leviticus he admitted that often when he went to his study each morning the thought of tackling Leviticus again weighed him down. John persevered and eventually realised that 'The laws of Leviticus are *meant* to weigh us down.' The exactness of details is intended to show us our weakness and inability to keep the holiness required by God, and this will lead us to the grace of forgiveness—and, in our case, to Christ.

It will help us to keep two important facts in mind: First, the book is about God and his offer of salvation, and therefore about Jesus Christ—we must look for him here.

Second, God's purpose in some of the detail is to keep his chosen people separate and different from the surrounding nations. Israel was intended to reveal the true God to an idol-worshipping world. Leviticus was evangelistic. God expressed this through Moses to Israel:

'I have taught you decrees and laws as the LORD my God commanded me, so that you may follow them in the land you are entering to take possession of it. Observe them carefully, for this will show your wisdom and understanding to the nations, who will hear about all these decrees and say, "Surely this great nation is a wise and understanding people." What other nation is so great as to have their gods near them the way the LORD our God is near us whenever we pray to him? And what other nation is so great as to have such righteous decrees and laws as this body of laws I am setting before you today?' (Deuteronomy 4:5–8).

The references in the Old Testament to 'the foreigners residing among you' (Leviticus 18:26) is evidence that there were those who recognised life among the Israelites was far more attractive than their native pagan society.

The approach in these daily devotions is very different from a commentary that discusses the details and analyses the meaning of words and phrases. This is a meditation and application on the main theme of each passage. In three months of daily readings, we can understand why this book is so important in the Bible, how it fits with the developing theme of redemption, and what the relevance is for a Christian today. We can enjoy reading this book, and not simply wade through so many details which may appear meaningless for a modern society. This is a simple introduction and a preparation for any deeper study.

Leviticus contains many careful and repeated details of sacrifices and offerings; to God and his people they mattered immensely, therefore to us they must not be tedious. Leviticus also contains instructions on intimate and sensitive matters; to God and his people these were holy things, therefore to us they must not be offensive. Some of the warnings and judgments are severe; to God and his people these were very necessary, therefore to us they must not seem unkind.

The repetition that occurs throughout Leviticus will mean there is repetition in application also. But that is God's design. Every teacher knows the value of repetition, repetition, repetition. Peter understood this well: 'I will always remind you of these things, even though you know them and are firmly established in the truth you now have. I think it is right to refresh your memory' (2 Peter 1:12–13). And so did Paul: 'I already gave you a warning when I was with you the second time. I now repeat it while absent' (2 Corinthians 13:2).

Like every book of the Bible, Leviticus is about God. As the singing birds and opening buds reveal the character of spring, so the ceremonies and civil laws reveal the character of God. But it is also a book about us—our defiling sin, our certain hope of salvation, and our need to live in a society governed by regulations. The civil code—dealing with marriage, health, property, employment, wealth, poverty and crime—reveals God's view of an ordered society.

However, Christ is everywhere in focus as we read through Leviticus. With minds that are spiritual and eyes that are fixed upon Christ, we can read Leviticus with profit. The good news of salvation is here. We do well to recall the encouragement given by Paul: 'Everything that was written in the past was written to teach us, so that through the endurance taught in the Scriptures and the encouragement they provide we might have hope' (Romans 15:4).

Day 1   Leviticus 1:1–2

The Author's signature

The authority of our book is here

1 'The LORD called to Moses'. What follows is not the primitive superstition of an ignorant nomadic tribe; it is the voice of the covenant God to his chosen people. The Jews generally refer to this book by a one-word title *Wayikrah*, which occurs fifty-six times throughout the book and gives us the opening phrase of the book, literally: 'And he called'. We are wise to listen to what the LORD said to Moses.

The context of our book is here

In Exodus God thundered law from Sinai. In Leviticus he spoke grace from the 'tent of meeting'. Law prepares us for grace as one breath prepares for the next. The two are inseparable, the alternative is death. What God spoke from the tabernacle was more comforting than that which he spoke from the mountain, but it was not more necessary. In Exodus God set free his people from slavery, in Leviticus he called them into fellowship. Communion follows liberation as summer follows spring.

The human writer of the book is here

According to Leviticus, Moses wrote the words that God gave him. Modern critics are equally certain he did not, and that these laws were set down nearly one thousand years later during the time of Ezra and Nehemiah; apparently the priests, losing popularity, tried to revive their prestige by pretending these laws were written by Moses! The eternal Son of God is our final court of appeal. he called it 'the Law of Moses' (Luke 24:44), declared that Moses spoke of him (John 5:46,47), and claimed that a command found only in Leviticus 14:1–32 came from Moses (Matthew 8:4).

The theme of our book is here

'Your offering' is central to the whole book. William Romaine, preaching in London in the eighteenth century, called it 'The gospel according to Leviticus'. So it is. We are tempted to pass over this book because it is full of sacrificial details and moral demands, but that is its glory, and why it is the Old Testament gospel. The true gospel is both salvation and morality, forgiveness and holiness. There will be many kinds of offering described in this book, but the most important of all are those for sacrifice: 'an animal from either the herd or the flock.'

God spoke of:

'Good things that are coming—not the realities themselves.'
(Hebrews 10:1)

Day 2 Leviticus 1:3–9

Setting and sacrifice

We are tempted to pass over Leviticus because its context seems far removed from our society. Written for a nomadic people over three thousand years ago it can surely have little to say to us today. The combustion engine was invented over one hundred and fifty years ago, but we did not abandon it as we moved into deeper scientific fields, we simply applied the old principles to new machines. Notice here:

The place
That which made the door of the tent of meeting a holy place was its distance from the world and its nearness to God. There could be no idolatry here, only a holy transaction. Golgotha where Christ died was outside the city of humanity's rejection, outside the smallness of our understanding, outside the brevity of our history—but close to the heart of God.

The offering
Here is a man with an offering to a holy God. No one can or dares to come alone; they must come with a sacrifice. Not any sacrifice, but a prescribed sacrifice. God's prescription is exclusive, there is no other remedy. That which was offered had to be perfect. The lame and the blind, the spotted and blemished, could all be killed and eaten, but not here. Every flawless animal sacrifice pointed to the ultimate and only sacrifice for sin. A signpost is not a destination.

Noble men have died for others,
Martyrs' blood for God has spilled.
But their place was not at Calvary,
Someone perfect there was killed.

The sinner's hand lay across the animal's head. Not its back, for sin is not merely a burden to bear; nor its heart, for sin is not a weakness of affection. But across its head, for sin is a deliberate violation of that which we know to be true.

The result
'Atonement' means a covering. God accepts that which is covered by the blood of the sacrifice. Wrath turns into mercy. He covers all our sin. Notice the phrase: 'pleasing to the LORD'. God wants

to receive his forgiven people back into a new relationship with himself; he wants to find pleasure in those once alienated from him. That is the purpose of atonement.

'The precious blood of Christ ... a lamb without blemish.'
(1 Peter 1:19)

Day 3   Leviticus 1:10–17

The burnt offering

In the whole burnt offering, not only the herdsmen and shepherds could come with their offering, even the poorest family could bring a pigeon. Poverty never excludes anyone from forgiveness, and wealth never admitted anyone. In the burnt offering the whole sacrifice was burnt. No portion was retained for food, and that was costly for a poor man. Our Saviour offered himself wholly in sacrifice; he retained no rights and demanded no concessions. The Father hid his face, and the sun hid its light; Christ was completely abandoned by heaven and earth. He was alone.

It was a messy sacrifice. It was meant to be. Sin is no light, clean matter; and neither is its punishment. The slaughterhouse is not a pleasant place; an abattoir is not for the squeamish. Blood and torn flesh, flies and the burning sun all made for an offensive scene. Pierced, crushed, wounded:

'He had no beauty or majesty to attract us to him, nothing in his appearance that we should desire him. He was despised and rejected by men, a man of sorrows, and familiar with suffering. Like one from whom men hide their faces … It was the LORD's will to crush him and cause him to suffer' (Isaiah 53:2–3, 10).

In 1528 William Tyndale wrote of Christ's sacrifice: 'God sent him into the world to bless us, and to offer himself for us a sacrifice of sweet savour, to kill the stench of our sins, that God should henceforth smell them no more, nor think on them anymore.'

The cruel agony of the cross is an offence to the tidy minds of respectable religionists, but the stench of crucifixion became an aroma pleasing to the LORD.

'Christ loved us and gave himself up for us as a fragrant offering and sacrifice to God.'

(Ephesians 5:2)

Day 4   Leviticus 2:1–10

The grain offering

The grain offering was bloodless and therefore was not an atonement. The Hebrew word is literally 'a gift or present' (*minchah*). Flour and oil represented the basic fruit of hard work; they were the staple diet and without them the nation would die. The grain offering, whether it was baked, grilled or fried, represented all that the worshipper possessed. What we offer to God will vary according to our wealth, culture or ability, but it must represent our all.

An old Indian custom was for a wealthy host to offer his guest a silver coin as a token that all his possessions were at the guest's disposal. In giving the part he offered the whole. By bringing our tithes and offerings to God we dedicate not just that which we give, but also that which we retain. It is an acknowledgement that all we have is his bounty and his possession.

The grain offering came after the burnt offering. We must not confuse the two or reverse the order. Never can our offering be a payment for sin; we may give up all our worldly possessions, forgo our dearest pleasure, and even hand over our life, but not one small stain of sin will be covered this way.

Dwight L. Moody, the American evangelist of the nineteenth century, once declared: 'I freely admit salvation is worth working for; it is worth a man going round the world on his hands and knees, climbing its mountains, crossing its valleys, swimming its rivers, going through all manner of hardship in order to attain it. But we do not get it that way.'

We work *from* the cross, not *to* it. That was Cain's great mistake in Genesis 4. He thought the fruit of his own toil would be sufficient; Abel was wiser in coming with the burnt offering first.

The grain offering was sprinkled with the fragrant odour of frankincense. It is a picture of prayer. An offering, unaccompanied by a humble prayerful spirit is wholly unacceptable to God. After the sweet smell of the atoning sacrifice comes the sweet smell of his people's prayerful offering.

'Golden bowls full of incense, which are the prayers of the saints.'
(Revelation 5:8)

Day 5 — Leviticus 2:11–16

The grain offering—salt, not yeast

Yeast (leaven) and honey cause fermentation. Decay and corruption are brought to all with which yeast comes into contact. We ought never to be content if there is an admixture of corruption in anything we offer to God. To bring our gifts with a heart of greed or our life with a mind of complaint is like adding yeast to the grain offering. The whole will be tainted. One drop of poison in a glass will ruin the whole drink.

On the other hand, salt is a vital preservative. In the East salt is still a symbol of an abiding covenant; the Arabic word for 'salt' is the same as an 'agreement' or 'treaty', and Arabs will eat together food with salt in token of an agreement. The phrase 'unfaithfulness to the salt' was once common. For the salt of God's unchanging covenant to be present, the leaven of sin and the sweetness of the world's lure must be absent. God is never unfaithful to the salt, but if we play with sin, he will not hear us. We must never presume upon his faithfulness. Have we forgotten the salt of our first devoted commitment to him?

The offering of the firstfruits represented the first and the best of the harvest. The Lord did not receive that which was left over at the end of the year, but that which came first—before the family was fed or the barn was stocked. It represented our gratitude for God's goodness. If what we give to God is holy, then the whole of our life will be acceptable to him: 'If the part of the dough offered as firstfruits is holy, then the whole batch is holy; if the root is holy, so are the branches' (Romans 11:16).

Now join with the wise and worship this child;
bring gifts that are fitting for him.

Not gifts that are rare, or what we can spare,
but all that we are—to the King!

Part of the offering was reserved for the priests, but the whole with the frankincense ascended to God. Others may share our wealth, but God alone will have our worship.

'She put in everything she had.' (Mark 12:44)

Day 6 — Leviticus 3:1–5

The fellowship or peace offering

The Hebrew word is *shelamim*, which is best rendered by peace or thank offering.

In the burnt offering and grain offering the sacrifice belonged entirely to God; no portion was retained by the offerer. But the peace offering was different. The whole was offered to God, but God gave back a part. God threw a banquet for his people to celebrate their reconciliation to him. It was a sacrifice of thanksgiving (Leviticus 7:15).

An invitation to a meal is universally a token of friendship. But unlike pagan feasts where men entertain the gods, the Lord was the host at the peace offering. On the basis of the shed blood of the sacrifice, he invited his reconciled people to a meal of friendship. 'You prepare a table before me' (Psalm 23:5). The peace offering was placed on top of the burnt offering (v. 5). That speaks well of the New Covenant. The Christian is a friend of God and should enjoy that relationship, but should never forget that the privileges of reconciliation lay upon the dying embers of the burnt offering.

There is a price to the privilege. There is no peace without Christ's death. Christian, go into this day as a friend of God, reconciled and at peace with him; God wants it that way and Christ died to make it so.

As God invited his people to this sacrifice of thanksgiving, so he has prepared a simple meal for the Christian to remember the privilege and the cost of atonement. Our presence at the LORD's Supper is by his invitation. We are the guests, Jesus Christ is the host—and Golgotha is the card upon which the invitation is written.

And there is a feast yet untasted. The table is spread, the places are reserved, the King is ready for his guests. We wait only for the heavens to part and for the Prince of Glory to ride out with his company of angels and call to his elect people with a voice that will be heard from north to south and east to west: a call that will bring joy to every Christian heart, the sweetest words ever to break into human history:

'Come, for everything is now ready.'   (Luke 14:17)

Day 7   Leviticus 3:6–17

The fellowship offering—the best is God's

The fat and the blood were prohibited as food. The fat parts mentioned here were considered the most nutritious and the most delicious, but the blood was the most precious. It was a symbol of the loss of a life. In the sacrifice of Christ there are many benefits that he gladly shares with his people: 'Everything I have is yours' (Luke 15:31). Forgiveness, cleansing, friendship, eternal life, peace and joy, are some of the sweet meats of his sacrifice that we can enjoy. But the best part of his sacrifice he can never share. The suffering, agony and shed blood together with the putrid corruption of our sin and the fierce wrath of a holy God, these are the fat portions that belong to him alone. He shares that which we can enjoy but he cannot share that which we could never bear.

Christ has not abolished Leviticus; he has fulfilled it (Matthew 5:17). The New Testament contains around forty references to Leviticus. If this book is the shadow of Christ, then why do we trouble to look at the shadow when we have the full light of the Son of God? Because no picture is complete unless it contains both lights and shades, and Leviticus highlights the coming Messiah and the privileges of the New Covenant people. Shadows are intended to enhance, not obscure.

Through the sacrificial laws, Abraham saw Christ (John 8:56) and so did Moses (John 5:46 and Hebrews 11:26). Even though he stood on the shadow side of the cross, if he had the eye of faith an Israelite could see the Messiah in the ceremonies. In the same way, we stand on the shadow side of heaven with shadowy images of our future described in the New Testament. Now we see dimly and in part (1 Corinthians 13:12 and Colossians 2:17), but with faith we can see into the reality of our future inheritance. Faith makes the substance substantially real (Hebrews 11:1). It was this reality of faith that made the services and duties enshrined in this book such a joy to the believing Israelite:

'How lovely is your dwelling-place, O LORD Almighty!
My soul yearns, even faints, for the courts of the LORD;
my heart and my flesh cry out for the living God.'
(Psalm 84:1–2)

Day 8   Leviticus 4:1–12

The offering for unintentional sin by the priest

Before we consider the nature of these 'unintentional sins', notice who first is mentioned as guilty (v. 3). The priest is the one 'appointed to represent them in matters related to God' (Hebrews 5:1). Under the new covenant of Christ, we no longer require a priest to offer our sacrifices and worship to God, but we have pastors and elders who minister God's word and God's care (Hebrews 12:7,17). They are men, and therefore with the same sinful nature and liability to failure and sin as anyone else. This is a reason for weakness—but never an excuse.

It was the priest who was the first to recognise sin, the first to own it, and the first to show up at the tent of meeting to demonstrate repentance and seek forgiveness. Spiritual leaders are called to be an example in righteousness and in repentance. Their responsibility before the people is great and therefore their sin is the greater. They need much prayer.

God appointed men, not angels, to lead his people. Because of their own frail humanity they would fully understand and identify with the weakness of those they served. Like the sinless High Priest they foreshadowed, God intended his priests to be pastors and not merely administrators.

'Every high priest is selected from among men ... He is able to deal gently with those who are ignorant and are going astray, since he himself is subject to weakness.'

(Hebrews 5:1–2)

Day 9 — Leviticus 4:13–21

The offering for unintentional sin by the community

Ignorance of the law is never an excuse for breaking it. So it is with God's law. Sin is serious and ignorance does not excuse or cancel guilt. Both ignorant and wilful rejection are equally sin.

Israel understood there is both individual and community guilt. The 'whole Israelite community' assembled to confess its sin. A local church family may live for years in violation of God's holy standard. The Christian community may slide into spiritual lethargy or irreverence in worship; they may overlook the needs of a member or neglect the fearful state of the unsaved in their neighbourhood; they may organise and govern their church contrary to God's word or accept a teaching that violates the truth. They may do all this unthinkingly, not deliberately but in ignorance. When at last God's word draws attention to it, there are two things they must at once remember:

First, unintentional sins are sin. Beware of the indifferent shrug or the excusing voice. When the whole congregation of Israel sinned ignorantly, they had to assemble and face the seriousness of their guilt. Perhaps we should pray more often for God to reveal to us our unintentional sin, and confess unknown sin more frequently.

Second, just as the congregation, through the elders, laid their hands upon the head of the animal of sacrifice, so a whole church can find forgiveness in the blood of Christ. A church, like an individual, can bemoan its sin for ever, but that does not remove it. When sin is confessed, we must leave it with Christ. The bull was carried 'outside the camp' (vv. 11,12); the people could see their sin disappearing into the wilderness. It is right for a church to repent, confess and feel ashamed of its corporate sin of lethargy or disobedience—but not for ever. Christ's sacrifice removes the sin away from the community. We must leave it there because he has.

'Jesus also suffered outside the city gate in order to make the people holy through his own blood.'

(Hebrews 13:12)

Day 10   Leviticus 4:22–26

The offering for unintentional sin by the leader

From the priests to the leaders there is the same weight of responsibility. Perhaps leaders, more than anyone else, are liable to this and more guilty when they fail. A thoughtless word or action, a careless example or casually irreverent attitude; even ignoring the quiet plea for help in the rush of a busy life, a leader may, unintentionally, cause someone to stumble or be offended, either in the church family or in the workplace. A soldier may walk into an ambush, but an officer leads his men there. A leader cannot sin by himself, even when the sin is unconscious.

'Let not many of you become teachers, my brethren, for you know that we who teach shall be judged with greater strictness' (James 3:1).

Others are watching. A duckling learns from its parents to swim, and a lion cub learns from its parents to kill. Both learn from watching, but the end is very different. God singled out the ruler, because unwitting sin will lead many more into the same actions.

No leader, whether political or religious, can be allowed to excuse themselves for a public offence on the grounds that it is overlooked when 'ordinary people' do the same. If a leader does not lead well, they are better to step down. Although leaders are more liable to unintentional sin, they should strive to be less capable of it. It would be a sad day for Israel when the rulers were offering sacrifices for unwitting sins more frequently than the people, because the leader, more than all, should know what is right and wrong. Spiritual and moral ignorance may fit for leaders in our modern society, but never in the community of God's people. 'If anyone's gift is to lead, do it diligently' (Romans 12:8).

'Pray for us. We are sure that we have a clear conscience and desire to live honourably in every way.'

(Hebrews 13:18)

Day 11   Leviticus 4:27–35

The offering for unintentional sin by the member

The Christian, and particularly the young Christian, will certainly offend God's holiness many times in a day without realising it. We may use language or engage in an action that only later we learn was wrong. We may tumble into sin without thinking, without warning and without knowing. In the pressure of business, the urgency of a crisis or the chaos of a family upset we may sin unwittingly and only later our conscience stabs us into regret. Our attitude, that we thought was so justified, we now see was wrong; our words, that we thought so controlled, we now appreciate were cruel and heated. Perhaps, on one issue or another, we have only just learnt what the Scripture teaches, and we had no idea our behaviour was wrong.

For however long we have walked with Jesus, every day of our lives—and many times a day—we will fall below the standard a holy God expects of his people. In a thousand ways we will sin without realising. We ignore the quiet prompting of the Spirit or in our busy rush overlook the needs of another; we brush aside the opportunity to speak for our Saviour or help a stranger. And all without a thought. What can we do when we never realised either at the time or later that we offended our God?

We will not despair but run to the cross and 'lay our hand on the head of the sin offering'.

'My faith would lay her hand
On that dear head of Thine,
While like a penitent I stand,
And there confess my sin.'

In all this, there is no invitation to launch a personal or community witch-hunt for unknown and unintentional sins. However, we must always humbly be ready to be 'made aware' (vv. 14, 23, 28) of any unthinking sin in our life. Parents do not expect their children to understand bad behaviour all at once, they reveal little by little. Similarly, when our heavenly Father teaches us, he does expect us to learn. Otherwise, the unaware sin of today will become the wilful disobedience of tomorrow.

'The blood of Jesus, his Son, purifies us from all sin.'   (1 John 1:7)

Day 12 — Leviticus 5:1–6

The sins of silence and defilement

The sin offering of the previous chapter covered those sins committed in ignorance. The offering in this chapter refers both to these and to deliberate and wilful sins. There is forgiveness even for these. Sadly, their name and number is legion and here God reminded his people of a sample.

The cowardly silence (v. 1)

To refuse to act as a witness when required is as bad as giving a false statement. British courts have the power to compel a witness to testify. We may sin not only in what we do say, by a lie or hurting a character, but also in what we do not say, by refusing to reject slander and gossip or defend someone against false or cruel accusations. We can sin by a cowardly silence when Jesus and Christian standards are smeared.

The unclean contact (vv. 2–3)

Regulations regarding clean and unclean animals will come later. Sufficient at present to remember that certain situations made the Israelite 'unclean'. There was a natural reason for this in health and hygiene, but there was also a spiritual reason. This uncleanness pictured the defilement of the world.

Daily we 'rub shoulders' with the world. We watch or read the news, hear the conversation, see the lifestyle, and slowly absorb the mind-set of those around us. We are unknowingly influenced by the corruption of an evil world. Sometimes we feel it and sometimes we don't. The grime of industry and commerce doesn't settle in a billowing cloud upon the fabric in our homes, but it filters in, little by little. Just so the thinking and values of the world. Pray to be kept 'from being polluted by the world' (James 1:27).

The faithless promise (v. 4)
It is as bad to promise good and neglect it, as to plan evil and perform it. It is an evil thing to promise anyone or God what we have no intention or ability to carry out. Let our promises be scrupulously sincere.

'We have the mind of Christ' … *'Sin shall not be your master.'*
(1 Corinthians 2:16 and Romans 6:14)

Day 13   Leviticus 5:7–13

No one too poor

A lamb, two doves or two young pigeons or a tenth of an ephah of fine flour. An offering for the sins of silence and defilement allows even the poorest to come for forgiveness at a cost. The 'tenth of an ephah' was a small amount.

Of all the sacrifices in the Old Testament none points more clearly to the necessity of the shed blood of Christ than this passage. Hebrews 9:22 reminds us, 'Without the shedding of blood there is no forgiveness.' Yet here we learn that the poorest in Israel could bring a tenth of an ephah of fine flour as his sin offering 'and he will be forgiven'. The writer to the Hebrews was aware of this passage in Leviticus, so he carefully recorded that the law required '*nearly everything* be cleansed with blood'. He was aware that under the law no sin was forgiven by the blood of bulls or goats, lambs or pigeons or by a tenth of an ephah of fine flour. Paul expressed this vital truth like this:

'God presented him [Jesus] as a sacrifice of atonement, through faith in his blood. He did this to demonstrate his justice, because in his forbearance he had left the sins committed beforehand unpunished—he did it to demonstrate his justice at the present time, so as to be just and the one who justifies those who have faith in Jesus' (Romans 3:25–26).

By 'sacrifice of atonement' the translators have avoided the uncommon word *propitiation*. But that word in the Greek (*hilasterion*) is very specific: it refers to God's just anger against sin met and satisfied in the sacrifice of Christ. Paul makes clear that animals could never really bear the judgment that human sin deserved; they were only symbols of the One who alone could bear the weight of this. Sins could be forgiven before Christ's death, but the punishment remained for Christ to bear.

All sin that has ever or will ever be forgiven, for Jew or Gentile, then or now, is only dealt with by the punishment Jesus bore on the cross. Christ is the Old Testament sacrifice—no less than ours.

'Not all the blood of beasts on Jewish altars slain,
could give the guilty conscience peace or wash away its stain.
But Christ, the heavenly Lamb, takes all our sins away;
a sacrifice of nobler name, and richer blood than they.'

'How much more will the blood of Christ ... cleanse our consciences from acts that lead to death, so that we may serve the living God.'
(Hebrews 9:14)

Day 14   Leviticus 5:14–19
Sin against 'holy things'

Significantly, the warning and penalty for unintentional sin against God's way of worship is more severe. Sacrilege—defiling that which is sacred—is the older name for it. No sin can be worse than that of trampling underfoot 'the LORD's holy things'. It may be done knowingly or unknowingly. It is sin either way. During the revival in the reign of King Hezekiah, the enthusiasm of the people led them to eat the Passover feast 'contrary to what was written'. Their hearts and motives were right because their zeal was for God, but their omission was sin, and they needed pardon (2 Chronicles 30:18–20). Doubtless Uzzah was sincere in steading the Ark, but his sincerity did not excuse his 'irreverent act' (2 Samuel 6:6–7).

The origin of the word *worship* is the value we give to someone—*worth-ship*. We too may commit sacrilege against God's way of worship—not intentionally, as the vandal who breaks up a service or destroys a place of worship, but in our spiritual activity. Is sacrilege the idle and wandering mind during public prayer or preaching, and the habit of arriving late for a service? Is sacrilege heard in the trivial chatter before or during our worship? Or in the splendid singing of a tune with no thought for the words? Christians do not normally lie or make false promises—but they do sing them in their hymns and songs. Is sacrilege hearing God's word to our mind and ignoring it; or promising a friend we will pray and forgetting it?

Sacrilege is withholding God's 'tithe' from the offering or my life and my gifts from his service. Sacrilege is talking cheaply to God or about God, or not talking to him at all. Sacrilege is pious talk without a holy life, or a holy life without a pure heart.

Sacrilege is many things, but sacrilege is always sin. God wants his people's worship to be pure, because as we worship, so we will live.

'You are a chosen people, a royal priesthood, a holy nation, a people belonging to God.'

(1 Peter 2:9)

Day 15   Leviticus 6:1–7

Honesty in everything

Abusing a trust, stealing and extortion, may be common in this world (v. 3 'any such sin that people may commit') but it is sin. To lose or break that which we borrow, and fail to repay, is wrong. To steal time or goods from our employer is wrong. To exact more than is right or fair in our business dealings is not shrewd or smart, it is wrong. To avoid a fare or entrance fee is wrong. Our expenses claims, tax returns, false change and underpayment, finding and keeping a lost item—all these are tests of our honesty in everything. God expects his people to be a society of scrupulous honesty and trust, unlike the surrounding nations.

They are not simply offences against society, they are 'unfaithful to the LORD' (v. 2). All sin is directed against God. It is neither unsocial behaviour nor psychological inadequacy. It is sin, and sin is a violation of God's law and God's character. It is God who makes wrong, wrong—not society.

When David finally came to repentance after abusing Bathsheba, murdering her husband, compromising the commander of his army and scandalising the nation (2 Samuel 11–12) he fell down before God and cried: 'I have sinned against the LORD.' Later David publicly confessed to God, 'Against you, you only, have I sinned and done what is evil in your sight' (Psalm 51:4). That is true repentance.

Restitution and compensation (v. 5) is the only adequate way in which we should pay society for the sin of dishonesty. Perhaps we should return to the wisdom of this as a nation. But how can anyone pay for their crime before God? They cannot. They must go back to the sacrifice and offer the guilt offering as a substitute.

In January 1977 Gary Mark Gilmore was executed by firing squad in the Utah State Prison for two cold-bloodied murders. It is reported that he refused to appeal the death sentence on the grounds that only his death could atone for his crime of murder. His death made history and led to a novel and a film. How tragically wrong was Gary Gilmore:

'Your death, not mine, O Christ,
has paid the ransom due;
ten thousand deaths like mine
would have been all too few.
Your righteousness, O Christ,
alone can cover me;
no righteousness but yours
suffices for my plea.'

'So that in all things God may be praised through Jesus Christ. To him be the glory and the power for ever and ever. Amen.'
(1 Peter 4:11)

Day 16 — Leviticus 6:8–13

The perpetual burnt offering again

We met the burnt offering first on day three. Whenever the Israelites stood at the door of their tents in the wilderness and looked towards the tabernacle there were two things that would arrest their attention. Above the Holy Place, in the sky between heaven and earth, God placed a large cloud to remind the people of his perpetual presence to 'guide them on their way' (Exodus 13:21–22). Their gaze would also settle on a wisp of smoke ascending from the altar of burnt offering. The cloud above was a message of friendship, but the column from the altar was a warning of judgment and death. Promises and warnings are equally messages of kindness.

There was something awesome, even frightening, in the smoke of the altar: an animal had been slaughtered and its body consumed by fire. It was there because God hated sin, and it was there perpetually (v. 12); three times God emphasised that the fire must be kept burning. Sin is a perpetual offence to a holy God, but the rising smoke was a reminder that the benefit of the sacrifice lasts for ever. There was a terrifying alternative to the smoke of the altar of burnt offering: for the unbelieving and unrepentant 'the smoke of their torment rises for ever and ever' (Revelation 14:11). The smoke of the burnt offering was the smoke of God's holy anger against sin.

Early in the morning the Israelite could watch the priest leave the tabernacle and carry the ashes from the altar through the camp to a clean place 'outside the camp'. They were carried through the camp so that all might see that the fire had consumed the offering; the cost of forgiveness had been paid.

The true cause for Christ's death on the cross is not medical—those who suffered the brutality of crucifixion always died—but theological. He who came to take the punishment for our sin must have died. Christ was the only person ever to walk planet earth who did not have to die. He chose to die.

'The death he died, he died to sin once for all; but the life he lives, he lives to God.'

(Romans 6:10)

Day 17   Leviticus 6:14–23

The grain offering again

We return to the grain offering introduced on day four; this time it is for the priests. Of all the smells discovered, few are so pungent or persistent as smouldering tobacco, and few are so contagious! Those who smoke smell, whether they intend it or not. They may smoke a little or a lot, but either way the smell betrays them. It penetrates their breath, skin and clothes and permeates their home and children. The priest would pour a sweet-smelling incense over his grain offering to make it 'an aroma pleasing to the LORD'. As with the earlier grain offering, it represented giving all to God.

Such an offering made men holy in the sight of God, not for a covering over of sin—that was the burnt offering—but representing a humble heart and a pure life. The absence of yeast in his grain offering made it free from all contamination. When we offer God ourselves and our possessions without reserve, this becomes not merely a pleasing aroma to him, but a powerful preventative also. Whoever encounters such people is greatly influenced by them (v. 18). It is hard to be foul in the face of purity; it is difficult to blaspheme in the presence of a tongue seasoned with grace. How much sin is restrained by the presence of Christians will never be known until the unbelieving world wakes up in eternity without them.

But we must not offer to Christ that which we have no intention of paying should the Lord decide to invest our promise. He has a right to everything, and he may demand it. Christ endangers our possessions on earth but love for the world endangers our prospects in eternity.

When the priests were set apart for their service, they offered half in the morning and half in the evening (v. 20). It is better to offer Christ our possessions often and remember, than to offer them once and forget. Those who would serve him most effectively will repeat their promises most often.

Christmas Eve 1964, as Margaret Hayes was facing death as a prisoner of the Congolese Simba rebels, she closed the book she had been reading and reflected upon its challenge to her faith. Margaret later wrote: 'That day in my room marked a spiritual crisis in my life. The Lord was teaching me to evaluate life in the light of the cross. Before, my consecration had not been complete; I had thought it had, but now I saw the superficialities. I asked to be crucified with my Lord. It would mean humiliation, degradation, self–denying and dying to self. The Lord was to show me how this was to be. He knows I prayed in all sincerity.' God spared Margaret's life.

'Thanks be to God, who always leads us in triumphal procession in Christ and through us spreads everywhere the fragrance of the knowledge of him.'

(2 Corinthians 2:14)

Day 18   Leviticus 6:24 – 7:10

Everything 'most holy'

The sin offering and the guilt offering are now repeated, but with something new in mind. Blood, representing the death of the sacrifice, were there in chapters 4 and 5, but now the word 'holy' occurs eight times—and almost ninety times throughout the book. Everything about the sacrifice was holy: clothing, containers, altar and priests. They were 'set apart' from the world and to the service of God. That is what *holy* means. But what made them holy was the 'sprinkled' blood of the sacrifice.

In the eyes of religion, holiness is often likened with being sprinkled with water, lighting a candle, donning the robes of a priest, saying prayers, reciting a creed, defending a cause, giving to the poor, believing in God or simply intending to do well. But holiness is as likely to be gained by smiling at a passing cat as by offering such superstitions to the eternal Almighty and holy, holy, holy God. The Pharisees had all the above, yet still Christ condemned them (Matthew 23:13–33).

Nothing can ever be holy unless it is covered by the blood of the sacrifice. In reality holiness has no meaning apart from Christ's sacrifice on the cross. The word *holiness* must be written in blood or it will never be understood:

'There is a fountain filled with blood,
drawn from Immanuel's veins;
and sinners plunged beneath that flood
lose all their guilty stains.'

There is another focus in these verses. Unlike the sin and guilt offering for the people and community, this is now food for the priests and their male family members. But it was a ceremonial eating, and the ceremonial was always a picture of reality. When Jesus referred to himself as the bread of life, he went further: 'Unless you eat the flesh of the Son of Man and drink his blood, you have no life in you' (John 6:48–58). Although the priest was not to drink the blood of the sacrifice, was Jesus referring to this? Unless we make his death our own and accept the value of his sacrificial blood then we can have no eternal life.

Is this offensive? The world shudders and rejects it. Talk of death if you must; even sacrifice if you will, though offering is more polite. But blood is crude and harsh. Of course, there was nothing polite or refined in these ancient sacrifices—nor in the crucifixion. It is what the blood and torn flesh represents that makes us holy—the blood and body of the eternal Son of God. Let anyone deny this and they cannot be a Christian.

'Make every effort to live in peace with all men and to be holy; without holiness no-one will see the LORD.'

(Hebrews 12:14)

Day 19   Leviticus 7:11–18

Gratitude for everything

The peace offering in chapter 3 was the friendship feast between an Israelite and God; it spoke of a new relationship once made clean by the sacrifice of the burnt offering. But there were two kinds of peace offering: that which was offered out of gratitude for reconciliation to God, and that which was offered out of overflowing 'thankfulness'. The 'freewill offering' is first mentioned in Exodus 35:29 and 36:3. It was in addition to the mandatory 'tithe' which is introduced here in chapter 27.

Always we should have hearts of gratitude for our reconciliation through Christ, but there ought also to be times when we are abundantly grateful for everything. The farmer is glad of any harvest, but gladder still for an abundant harvest. All Christians say 'thank you' to God for his love, but few have a heart often bursting with praise and joy.

Where is the spontaneous thanksgiving? The heart that explodes with love? The visible and audible response of God's people? I have sometimes preached Christ with a full heart until I have felt tears gathering within me; and yet the congregation has sat neatly silent like tidy figures in the waxworks. A wise old missionary once offered his own cure for a cold heart: 'I praise God with my mouth and let my heart catch up later.' James offered his advice: 'Is anyone happy? Let them sing songs of praise' (James 5:13).

God now encouraged them to eat bread with yeast so that they would not think yeast, sometimes a symbol of rottenness, was in itself a bad thing. Look around at the incredible creation, mark the abundance of your possessions and the weight of your food store. Even if that fails you: with the eternal God as your Father, the eternal Christ as your Saviour and the eternal Spirit as your Counsellor, why should your praise not burst forth like a flood of water from the opening sluice gate? Someone wrote, 'Joy is the ensign that is flown at the citadel of the heart when the King is in residence.' God wants his people to be a thankful and happy people.

'Everything God created is good, and nothing is to be rejected if it is received with thanksgiving ... God, who richly provides us with everything for our enjoyment.'

(1 Timothy 4:4; 6:17)

The gospel according to Leviticus **33**

Day 20　　　　　　　　　　Leviticus 7:19–27

Care in worship

Our exuberance must not lead us into irreverence. Meat was good, but it must not be contaminated with corruption or enjoyed with what is forbidden. However solemn our demeanour or however excessive our performance, God is not pleased if it comes from a disreputable life. The silent contemplation of the Hindu wise man is no nearer the heart of true religion than the wild excesses of the tribal dance.

Let the worshipper examine the heart: 'If anyone who is unclean eats any meat of the fellowship offering belonging to the LORD, that person must be cut off from his people' (v. 20). If we are flirting with the world, seduced by sin, or dabbling in disobedience, then we have no right to sing of our reconciliation with God. It is true we may be reconciled, and the blood of the burnt offering may have covered our sin, but we have no right to presume upon the grace of God. If our life is currently a discredit to the gospel then we had better remain silent for a while. The drunken ambassador is still an ambassador, but until he is sober he would be well advised to talk little of his exalted office for he is hardly a credit to his Sovereign. The exuberant Christian with a disreputable life is plainly insulting the Lord.

The Jew was forbidden to eat the succulent fat or the nourishing blood of the sacrifice. These two were the best and the life. But they represented much more. The body and blood of Christ are holy things for the Christian. The elements of bread and wine in the Lord's Supper are not holy in themselves, and certainly no change takes place in them, but what they represent should make us treat the whole service with care. The Jew would eat judgment if he carelessly ate the peace offering, and so do we if we thoughtlessly and irreverently approach the Lord's Table—or any act of worship.

'Whoever eats the bread or drinks the cup of the Lord in an unworthy manner will be guilty of sinning against the body and blood of the Lord.'

(1 Corinthians 11:27–29)

Day 21   Leviticus 7:28–36
'With his own hands'

When any Israelite offered his sacrifice, he must come in person: 'With his own hand he is to present the offering … and wave the breast before the LORD.' This was an admission of his own guilt and acknowledgement of his own thankful dependence upon God.

The offering was a substitute but there could be no substitute for the offerer. If he would not come in person, he could not come at all.

In our modern society the necessity of *procuratia*—from the Latin word for 'proxy'—is often unavoidable. Proxy means that we ask someone else to act on our behalf, we delegate our responsibility and they become our substitute. Much is innocently unavoidable. We leave it with others to fight our wars, police our streets and sort out our chaotic political, industrial and economic problems. We even enjoy our sport by *procuratia*.

It is, of course, a catastrophe in the realm of training our children when parents abandon their responsibility to teach and direct their children in moral and social behaviour, or when the government takes this responsibility away from them.

Nowhere is this seen more dangerously than in the realm of religion. Multitudes rely on their Priest, Imam, Granthi, Lama or Guru to perform their religion for them. It is *religio procuratia*—religion by proxy. The comfortable reassurance that those more in tune with deity can do my religion for me, in life and death, and I need not trouble myself too much with personal commitment. The priest does it all for me.

It was once common for parents to send their children to church to learn Christianity by proxy, without bothering at home. By proxy Christians may be content to preach the gospel overseas through their missionaries and consider that their evangelism is done. By proxy we pray at the prayer meeting and remain silent.

The Christian faith is foremost a personal commitment to God through Jesus both for salvation and a life of godly service.

'Offer your bodies as living sacrifices, holy and pleasing to God—this is your spiritual act of worship.'

(Romans 12:1)

Day 22 — Leviticus 7:37 – 8:9

All is almost ready

The sacrifices and the offerings have been described and God's people are familiar with what is required. But who will offer the sacrifices? Not just anyone may come forward to act as priest for the people. Aaron and his four sons were called out and set apart for this high office. They represented Christ who was both Priest and Sacrifice. The way of salvation was planned in eternity, but the day came when Christ could say, 'Here I am—it is written about me in the scroll—I have come to do your will, O God' (Hebrews 10:7). As Aaron looked over the congregation of Israel gathered around the tabernacle, he could surely use the words that would later be in the mouth of our Lord: 'Here am I, and the children God has given me' (Hebrews 2:13).

However, Aaron was only a man, and he must be ordained to this office in order to impress upon him, his sons, their descendants and all the people, that to act in any degree as a representative of God is an awful responsibility. Everything in this ordination must show that Aaron represented that which is holy and undefiled. The congregation must see this.

Symbolically Aaron and his sons were washed and re-clothed. Every part of Aaron's clothing was significant: his coat, girdle, robe, ephod, breastpiece, Urim and Thummim, turban and golden plate. They are detailed in Exodus 28–29. Of the nine items we will take here only three.

The robe covered his own garments as the righteousness of Christ covers our sinful humanity.

The breastpiece of decision (Exodus 28:29), containing the names of the twelve tribes of Israel, brought them continually before God who remembered his covenant with his chosen people as Christ presents his elect before the Father.

The golden plate was engraved with the words 'Holy to the Lord' and worn on the forehead of the priest who 'will bear the guilt involved in the sacred gifts the Israelites consecrate … It will be on Aaron's forehead continually so that they will be acceptable to the Lord' (Exodus 28:38). Christ came to make us holy and to hold that holiness for ever before God so that nothing can ever again be laid against us.

'He himself bore our sins in his body on the cross.'   (1 Peter 2:24)

Day 23   Leviticus 8:10–13

The fragrant oil

When the fragrant oil ran down Aaron's hair, dripped from his beard and fell from his robe to the floor he had been anointed by God. But this oil was not commonplace. The instructions for its manufacture and detailed arrangements for its application were exclusive. No other oil was to be made like this, and this oil was to be used for nothing but the service of the tabernacle (Exodus 30:22–33). The anointing speaks of the presence of the Holy Spirit.

Salvation is as much the work of the Spirit as of the Son and the Father. The title *Christ* means 'the anointed one', and at his baptism the Holy Spirit came upon Jesus; the Father anointed him 'with the Holy Spirit and with power' (Acts 10:38). Jesus later claimed, 'The Spirit of the Lord is on me, because he has anointed me to preach good news to the poor' (Luke 4:18).

The fragrance of the oil is the harmony of Father, Son and Holy Spirit in their preparation and accomplishment of the way of salvation when all heaven bent to rescue rebel sinners from hell. Unlike Aaron, our Saviour did not require the Spirit to make up the deficiencies of his human nature; on the contrary, he required the Spirit to demonstrate that he worked on earth as he worked in heaven: in harmony with the Father and the Spirit. It was impossible for him to speak or act without the Spirit, not because of weakness, but because of his unity in the Godhead. A whale cannot live out of water, not because of weakness, but because of its nature. So, Jesus as the Son of Man and Son of God could not live without the Spirit.

There is a spirit of the world which is the spirit of Satan, and his agents are spirits of darkness. They live and breed around the foul stagnation of sin and, like the malarial mosquito, they inject death into the lifeblood of mankind. The spirits of evil bring fear, suffering, darkness. Untreated, the rigor of fever will become the rigor of death.

As the oil of anointing was unique, so is the Spirit of God; as the one was holy, so is the other. The Holy Spirit is pure and clean; he brings life, joy and usefulness. He conveys faith to our mind, Christ to our heart and salvation to our soul. All who are born again are sprinkled with both the blood and the oil. The Father and the Son, in the Person of the Spirit, have taken up residence in the life of every Christian: 'We will come to him and make our home with him (John 14:23). That is a fragrant oil, pure and clean—without it we cannot love him or serve him.

'Chosen according to the foreknowledge of God the Father, through the sanctifying work of the Spirit, for obedience to Jesus Christ and sprinkling by his blood.'

(1 Peter 1:2)

Day 24　　　　　　　　　　Leviticus 8:14–29

The part represents the whole

'The tip of his right ear, the thumb of his right hand and the great toe of his right foot.' In this symbolic act the whole of Aaron was covered by the blood of the sacrifice and set apart for the service of God. His ear would always be open to the voice of God, and his hands and feet ready for instant obedience. When Christ came, God prepared for his Son a body and he served his Father as man as well as God.

We can worship God in spirit only if we serve him with our body. Some Christians would perhaps be more use to God if they were angels in heaven, for it is certain that they are very little use to him as servants on earth. They are full of supposed worship, but empty of real action. The evangelical Christian is not one who merely gives a formal assent to the grand doctrine of a Bible without error, but one who, having given such assent, then lives up to it.

There are mammoths in London, complete with fur and tusks, but for all their apparent strength they are lifeless; mammoths became extinct a few thousand years ago and their patchwork remains in a museum. God has no use for showy but lifeless Christians. He is not curator of a museum but Creator of a living church. Unless God has the whole of our allegiance he may as well have none of it. An army that is partly loyal is worse than no army at all.

Has the blood of Christ touched your ears, your hands and your feet?

Moses placed in Aaron's hands a sample from each sacrifice and offering (vv. 25–27), and the priest held them up before the Lord. In offering the part, Aaron offered the whole. God rarely demands everything at once; but he demands something always. It is an idle debate whether or not I would respond to a call to the mission field, stand to be shot for my faith or give up my treasured possessions. The issue is what does God want from me today? If a soldier will not shine his boots, it is doubtful whether he will bother to clean his gun; and he will certainly not fight loyally for his country.

'You have been faithful with a few things; I will put you in charge of many things.'

(Matthew 25:21,23)

Day 25   Leviticus 8:30–36

Seven days of worship

Seven days in the tabernacle—and some Christians find two hours in church a heavy burden! It is true they did not dare to leave (v. 35), but did they want to? Is there any better place for the people of God than to be in the place of worship? When next you leave home for church with a cold heart and reluctant step, sing with the Psalmist: 'You, God, are my God, earnestly I seek you; I thirst for you, my whole being longs for you' (Psalms 63:1). And, like the wise old missionary, you may find that if you praise God with your lips your heart will catch up later. I doubt whether any Christians, on arrival in heaven, will file a petition requesting eternity be cut back in time.

There was no inactivity for Aaron and his sons. And why should there be? There is always plenty to be done in the service of worship. A busy heart is never bored. And what the LORD ordains is never tedious. When God urged his people to stop seeking their own pleasure on the Sabbath he promised them that they would learn to call the day 'a delight' (Isaiah 58:13). Apparently, Aaron and his sons did not complain; they looked more at the privilege than the problems; they enjoyed the worship, and the work became a pleasure.

Those seven days must have been the most precious in their lives. Everything was new and unfamiliar. Each day offerings were made, and they had not yet learned to take anything for granted. They had not yet become over familiar with holy things. It was like the springtime of conversion when everything is new and exciting. But the offerings during those seven days were strictly for Aaron and his sons. The people were not yet admitted.

Our High Priest is 'holy, blameless, pure, set apart from sinners, exalted above the heavens' (Hebrews 7:26). But not so these earthly priests. They were not fit to serve until they had personally learned the enormity of their sin and the magnitude of God's mercy. Daily, sacrifices were made, blood was shed, and animals were burned on the altar, but never could they say, 'It is for the people, they are so bad.' We can never offer Christ's forgiveness to others unless first we have felt it for ourselves; and we can never preach on the gravity of sin unless first we have felt it in ourselves.

'Unlike the other high priests, he [Christ] does not need to offer sacrifices day after day, first for his own sins, and then for the sins of the people.'

(Hebrews 7:27)

Day 26 Leviticus 9:1–21

Ready for the people

On day eight, for the first time, Aaron was to offer the sacrifices for the people. It was not the first time they were offered because Moses was a priest and had sacrificed for the people. Perhaps now some came with interest to see how the new man would manage. But curiosity is no way to worship and the fearsome solemnity of the service would soon put the dread of God into the idle spectator.

In this chapter the unalterable order of offerings is clearly seen. Whenever sacrifices were offered the order must be the same. First came the ***sin offering*** with its central thought of the cleansing of sin by the sprinkled blood. Second came the ***burnt offering*** (chapter 1) during which the whole of the sacrifice was burnt and not one portion retained for the worshipper or priest; this signified the satisfying of God's holy anger by the death of the sacrificial animal. The ***grain offering*** (chapters 2, 6) represented all that the offerer owned. Then came the ***fellowship offering*** (chapter 3) representing a feast of reconciliation with God.

Many look for lasting peace and joy, but the true cost is beyond anyone to purchase it. God accepted no other currency than the blood of the sacrifice representing his Son.

Aaron 'came to the altar' (v. 8). That was a bold step, but not a presumptuous one. Aaron knew that he had the right to draw near because he came with the sacrifice in his hands and nothing else. Simon the sorcerer (Acts 8) can number his followers by the millions of those who try to buy or barter their way into the good things of the kingdom by decency and good works. It cannot be done. We may come to God only by faith in the finished work of Christ on Golgotha. It is a privilege that those who will, may draw near to the altar of God's sacrifice.

'Let us draw near to God with a sincere heart and with the full assurance that faith brings.'

(Hebrews 10:22)

Day 27   Leviticus 9:22

'Aaron stepped down'

When Aaron 'stepped down' from the altar, it was because he could do no more. He had offered the symbols. It was Christ who accomplished the reality. When he came down from the cross, it was finished. All was accomplished.

Over the millennia of Israel's history, hundreds of thousands of bulls, sheep, goats and pigeons would be destroyed on the altar as a burnt offering, tons of fine flour and gallons of sweet oil would be used. Did the Jews ever consider it all a terrible waste? Sadly, they often did. At times they chose the blind and lame from the herds and flocks; at other times they offered nothing at all.

However, for the Jew who came with a true heart, the lamb that he carried to the tabernacle for himself and his family was the best that he had. It would have provided a valuable breeding ram or a substantial meal. The animal had consumed a large amount of lush pasture and fresh water, both scarce enough in the desert conditions of Israel's nomadic life in the wilderness. He had spent time and energy rearing it, and now it was to be handed over to be destroyed. Yet with the eye of faith he could never see it as a waste. Regularly he was reminded of the cost of reconciliation with his Creator. But he knew it was the only way.

Because Christ paid the penalty once and for all for sin and we bear no part of the price, we may treat sin the more lightly. It is no burden to us however much we sin! God demands none of our goods and no more of our money to pay the added value. Forgiveness is easy to obtain; we have only to ask.

Perish such thoughts! Are we disciples of Christ or of Judas? There are always those who dismiss the cross, the prayer meeting, and the service of Christ as 'Why this waste?'—of love, time and energy. Surely no Christian heart can play with sin and presume upon Christ. Using the present continuous tense, John the apostle comments: 'The one who does [and goes on doing] what is sinful is of the devil' (1 John 3:8).

Every Christian will sin, but here is the test: Does our conscience nag and our spirit sag? Do tears flow inwardly for the awful cost of the sinless Son of God becoming our vile and loathsome sin? We say that salvation is without price, and so it is. But it is not without cost. We must know the difference.

'Christ redeemed us from the curse of the law by becoming a curse for us.'

(Galatians 3:13)

Day 28   Leviticus 9:23–24

'The glory of the LORD'

The offerings were over and the day was almost at an end. It remained for the people to be blessed by the priest and for the offering to be accepted by God. Aaron lifted up his hands and the Lord sent down his fire. Aaron did not dispense a blessing to the people any more than he dispensed God's salvation. The Shekinah glory that Moses had seen on the mountain (Exodus 19:16–24) now filled the tabernacle. Later, God's glory came at the dedication of Solomon's temple (2 Chronicles 7:1–2). Then, as perhaps now, the priests could not stand before the splendour of God's presence.

But the Lord is no less among his chosen people today, and although our eyes may not be dazzled by his glory, our hearts may still be warmed by the touch of his Spirit. We ought never to meet without believing that he is near.

Whenever we are obedient to God there is always blessing. Whenever we are engaged in activities that focus upon God—whether baptism, the Lord's Supper, preaching, prayer or Christian fellowship—God comes down to his people and blesses them.

A significant phrase forms a fitting epilogue to the ordination of Aaron and his sons as high priest and priests: 'Fire came out from the presence of the LORD.' Fire came from God and burned up the offerings. The sacrifices were consumed by no ordinary fire. In no more striking way could the people be shown that the almighty and sovereign God had accepted the sacrifices by the fire of his just anger against sin.

It was an anger that would either consume the sacrifice or those who offered the sacrifice—a distinction the people were about to learn. God answered by fire: 'It is enough, I am satisfied.' The fire was God's 'Amen' upon every offering Aaron had made.

That also pointed forward to Golgotha when God's fierce anger turned on his Son. Only then could we breathe with relief in the knowledge that as lightning does not strike twice so God will punish sin once and once only. If Christ has taken my sin, then it is never possible for me to bear its guilt or punishment. When Christ cried out 'It is finished'—it was! Joy and fear mingle at the cross.

'We considered him punished by God, stricken by him, and afflicted … the punishment that brought us peace was on him … it was the LORD's will to crush him and cause him to suffer …'.

(Isaiah 53:4,5,10)

Day 29   Leviticus 10:1–2

'Unauthorised fire before the LORD'

Some parts of Scripture are particularly holy ground, and we walk across them with dread and awe. Only a fool treads carelessly through a minefield. This chapter is a spiritual minefield, therefore we will be wise to slow our pace and pick our way through it with caution.

Suddenly the fire of God fell again! As one preacher well expressed it, the priests were in the most dangerous job in the world! We need not enquire for the exact nature of the sin of Nadab and Abihu; 'contrary to his command' is enough. Were the precise details of God's instructions so very important? Clearly, yes. The atmosphere was spiritually charged, excitement and enthusiasm ran high; the people were ecstatic in their praise, and the priests were doubtless immersed in the atmosphere of worship.

We have no right to query the motives of Nadab and Abihu any more than those of Uzzah who similarly died for touching the Ark (2 Samuel 6), but the commands of God were clear. However, these were priests and they were in the act of worship. So they may have been, but sincerity is not sufficient. David Brainerd was sincere, and possibly quite right, when in 1741 he claimed that one of his tutors had 'no more grace than this chair', but for this indiscreet remark he was expelled from Yale College.

It is not enough for a man to be a minister, vicar, priest, bishop, or whatever other title he may carry. He must be holy. He may be successful, oversee a growing congregation, own a name honoured and applauded, but we dare not accept superficial judgements or be dazzled by impressions. James wisely warns: 'You know that we who teach will be judged more strictly' (James 3:1). There is often an unspiritual squeamishness about criticism; however, we are warned in Scripture against making our own judgements, but never against passing on God's judgements from his word.

The Christian leader especially, must be particular about sin; our conscience must be sensitive; we must be instant in our obedience to God's word. It is not what we feel or think the Spirit is saying that matters most; we must ask: 'What has the Lord commanded?'

> *'Does the LORD delight in burnt offerings and sacrifices*
>   *as much as in obeying the LORD?*
> *To obey is better than sacrifice,*
>   *and to heed is better than the fat of rams.'*
>
> (1 Samuel 15:22)

Day 30 Leviticus 10:3
'I will be proved holy ... I will be honoured'

Did Aaron consider the punishment hasty and unjust? Is there a note of complaint in David's response to the death of Uzzah: 'David was angry because the LORD's wrath had broken out against Uzzah' (2 Samuel 6:8)? What runs through our minds when we have a small view of God? God is wise and fair and always has a reason for everything he does.

God demonstrates his holiness in judgement. The magistrate who winks at a crime had better leave the bench. God is not only holy, he will be seen to be holy; and all who toy with sin and trample upon God's word will feel that he is holy. It is not for us to question his justice but to fall down and tremble before a God who will not tolerate sin.

'Among those who approach me'. If God is not seen to be holy among those who claim to be reconciled by Christ, then where else will his holiness be seen? The Romani 'Gipsy Smith' became an evangelist with the Salvation Army in 1877 and frequently sang: 'How shall the world know of Jesus unless it sees Jesus in me?' How will the world know of holiness unless his people are holy? And how will his people be holy unless his leaders are? Those who, by their calling spend much time at his throne and his word offer unholy fire if their lives are not holy.

The First Book of Discipline, drawn up in 1560 for the Presbyterian Church in Scotland contained the following instruction for ministers:

'That he with all careful diligence attend upon the flock of Christ Jesus, over which he is appointed pastor; that he walk in the presence of God so sincerely that the graces of the Holy Spirit may be multiplied unto him, and in the presence of men so soberly and uprightly, that his life may confirm in the eyes of men that which by tongue and word he persuaded unto others.'

This will do for pastor, elders, deacons, teachers, leaders ... all who are near him by the nature of their office and ministry. 'In the sight of all the people.' Hold up a mirror to the sun and you will set fire to the grass; paint the mirror black and nothing but a shadow is cast. When we cast a shadow across the path of a younger Christian our name is Nadab and Abihu. We must fire others with love for Christ by the holy reflection of our lives.

'Remember your leaders, who spoke the word of God to you. Consider the outcome of their way of life and imitate their faith.'
(Hebrews 13:7)

Day 31 — Leviticus 10:4–7

'They did as Moses said

We can be sure they did! A lesson was severely learned. If the priests were to take seriously the holiness of God, they must take seriously his judgments also. The people may weep over the death of Nadab and Abihu, but not the priests. They were to stand on the side of God and explain the necessity for such action.

We dare not treat our belief in eternal security as an indulgence for careless living. Has God ceased to discipline professing Christians for sin? Ananias and Sapphira died for dishonesty (Acts 5). Simon the sorcerer was warned of judgment for a heart 'full of bitterness and captive to sin' (Acts 8:23). When Hymenaeus and Alexander rejected their conscience, they made shipwreck of their faith and were delivered to Satan (1 Timothy 1:19–20). At Corinth, members of the church came flippantly and irreverently to the Lord's table: 'That is why many among you are weak and sick, and a number of you have fallen asleep' (1 Corinthians 11:30).

God will not tolerate sin among his people and will decimate a congregation if it refuses to accept his Lordship. When Nadab and Abihu died, forty per cent of the priesthood was buried. So be it. God would rather no priests than unholy priests. Was he setting the same standard in the sudden death of Ananias and Sapphira? The church under the new covenant must be holy no less than the church under the old. Is our slovenliness in worship a reason for the low level of spiritual life among many Christians and congregations today?

One of our greatest dangers is to forget that God has not changed. He may not always judge now as he did then, but to 'worship' with bitterness and resentment in the heart, disobedience or indifference in the soul, the world and its business in the mind, or the lusts of the flesh in the body, will inevitably lead to a weak and sickly Christianity. Do not weep at God's judgment, weep rather that he has cause to judge.

Watch the lifeless bodies of Nadab and Abihu carried through the camp, and tremble. God's righteous judgment will either consume the sacrifice—or those who offered it.

'If we were more discerning with regard to ourselves, we would not come under such judgment.'

(1 Corinthians 11:31)

Day 32   Leviticus 10:8–11
Distinguish between the holy and the common

Is this where the trespass of Nadab and Abihu was born? A little wine beclouded their judgement and led them to offend the holiness of God? Consequently, God set a commandment among his priests: They must abstain from any alcohol when they are on duty. 'An unnecessary strictness' declares the religious libertine. However, God commands nothing without good reason. It is doubtful that Nadab and Abihu were drunk, but it was likely their judgement was impaired. No-one knows the precise limit for themselves. There is nothing necessarily sinful in the 'common' or 'unclean', but not all things are beneficial. Those who are called to distinguish between the 'holy and the common' (the helpful and the unhelpful?) need a clear mind; those who are set apart to teach the word of God (v. 11) must be alert.

Even in a land where there was little else to drink, God commanded Aaron to abstain. What if the people saw Aaron and his sons a little unsteady? Abstention avoids the possibility. It may not be wrong to drink alcohol moderately, but God had good reason to order his priests to abstain.

'Wine is a mocker and beer a brawler; whoever is led astray by them is not wise' (Proverbs 20:1).

'It is better not to eat meat or drink wine or to do anything else that will cause your brother or sister to fall' (Romans 14:21).

'Whether you eat or drink or whatever you do, do it all for the glory of God. Do not cause anyone to stumble, whether Jews, Greeks or the church of God '(1 Corinthians 10:31–32).

One third of all prisoners in the United Kingdom admit to heavy drinking and sixteen percent are alcohol dependent. The World Health Organisation estimates that roughly half of those committing domestic abuse were drinking alcohol prior to assault. Five percent of all road accidents are alcohol related.

Were Nadab and Abihu confident they could drink wisely? Apparently not wisely enough. The 'common' thing gained mastery over them. Perhaps they were unsteady only once, but it was never forgotten. There are some things a Christian has only to do once but it will never be forgotten by the world or the congregation. And who would like to set an example that would begin a young Christian on the road to an addiction? There is only one guarantee to avoid this.

'"I have the right to do anything," you say—but not everything is beneficial. "I have the right to do anything"—but not everything is constructive. No one should seek their own good, but the good of others.'

(1 Corinthians 10:23–24)

Day 33   Leviticus 10:12–15

The funeral wake

There must have been an awful fear gripping the household of Aaron. With only two sons left, evidently Aaron was bewildered at God's sudden and fierce judgment and reluctant to continue with the offerings of the day in case, by a slip of obedience, he lost the rest of his family. In these verses Moses did nothing more than remind Aaron of the detail of the cereal (grain) offering. Apparently, this was the point of worship at which the fire had fallen, and the priests had abandoned their post. Moses now commanded them to go back to their work of doing what they knew to be right.

They must not allow one failure to become an excuse to cease worship or service.

At this very hour of mourning, the sons and daughters of Aaron were called to a feast of cakes and lamb. God provided the funeral wake. Was God comforting the family? The wake is also a time for remembering.

The instructions for the grain offering were repeated in brief. Millions of words and hours of sermons would be saved if we only needed to be told something once. But that has never been possible. Paul was aware of this when he wrote to the Philippians: 'It is no trouble for me to write the same things to you again, and it is a safeguard for you' (Philippians 3:1). When you catch yourself complaining inwardly: 'I've heard all this before,' ask, 'Has it changed my life yet? Is that why I need to be reminded?'

Aaron had forgotten his duty and Moses snapped him back to the task. Memory is the easiest facility to lose and the hardest to find; the more we store away in its vaults the less we seem able to recall. Ministry must keep on saying the same things until we stop forgetting what it said the first time. It is not irksome but safe.

'I will always remind you of these things, even though you know them and are firmly established in the truth you now have. I think it is right to refresh your memory ... I will make every effort to see that after my departure you will always be able to remember these things ... This is now my second letter to you. I have written both of them as reminders.'
(2 Peter 1:12, 13, 15; 3:1)

Day 34   Leviticus 10:16–18
Longing to be obedient

Then there was one! It almost looked as if Eleazar and Ithamar were now to be deposed and Aaron would remain the only priest. Their offence was a technical one. According to Leviticus 6:26–30 most sin offerings were to be eaten by the priests, but if, as in the case of a sin offering by a leader, the blood was sprinkled in the holy place, then the whole of the sacrifice was to be burnt. The sin offering here was for the people (v. 17) and therefore the animal should have been eaten.

Aaron was in a dilemma. Originally the offering was for the nation, and it should therefore have been priest's food; suddenly judgment had struck the sons of Aaron and he wondered whether it should now be considered a sin offering for the priest's family, in which case he could not allow his two remaining sons to eat it. Either way he may be wrong, and he dare not risk another offence. It was all so complicated.

Moses wisely let God be the judge and, apparently, Aaron had made a wise decision. Not every decision the Christian has to make is obvious or easy. However, God has written his law upon our hearts (Jeremiah 31:31–34 and Hebrews 8:8–13) so that when we are uncertain, he knows our intention. For the healthy Christian, the standards of God's word are not external legislation to be borne as a grudging duty but written upon the heart to be kept with joy and willingness. We should never use the commands of God as a legal scourge to keep us perpetually miserable, or dismiss their value and escape into the questionable freedom of a convicted prisoner at large.

Perhaps Aaron was unable to appreciate this at the present. However, David entered into some of the early joys of the New Covenant. Here are his expressions of love for God's Law in Psalm 119:

'I will praise you with an upright heart as I learn your righteous laws ... I rejoice in following your statutes as one rejoices in great riches ... How I long for your precepts ... I remember, LORD, your ancient laws, and I find comfort in them ... Oh, how I love your law! I meditate on it all day long ... I love your law ... I love your commands more than gold, more than pure gold ... Your promises have been thoroughly tested, and your servant loves them ... See how I love your precepts ... May my lips overflow with praise, for you teach me your decrees.'

We should never fall behind David in our love for the commands of God, or behind Aaron in our desire to keep them.

'In my inner being I delight in God's law.' (Romans 7:22)

Day 35   Leviticus 10:19–20

Confusing complexity!

Moses was not wrong to enquire of God, neither was Aaron wrong to defend his action. Sometimes we think all issues should be black or white; plainly right or wrong. That would simplify some problems, but multiply others and turn us into Pharisees. The six hundred and thirteen Pharisaic 'laws' built as a hedge around the Law of God, developed from this desire for simple solutions. But it led to a burdensome legalism.

Moses was right, and so was Aaron. Moses was correct by the letter of the law, but Aaron saw another principle had arisen that took precedence over the first. The sin of the nation was one thing, and for that there was one form of sin offering, but when sin came into his own family, Aaron rightly judged that this must be atoned for before he continued on behalf of the nation.

Beware those who never have a problem with what is right or wrong or have an instant solution to every issue. Infants make few decisions; parents tell them what to do and what not to do. As they grow older we expect them to learn what is right and wrong, good and bad, and slowly make right decisions in complex situations based on the principles we have taught them.

At school I always found maths hard, but my teachers never simply gave me the answers; they taught me the rules and principles and left me to work out the answers. That is the intention of God's word and law in the Bible.

Watch always for the higher principle that overrides the lower. This may well solve a dilemma. Public prayer and worship is good, and to neglect it is sin, but to leave it aside in order first to be reconciled with a fellow Christian is another principle that overrides the first (Matthew 5:24). Our God is not an unreasonable taskmaster; he knows the problems we face.

When Aaron explained his dilemma and the careful way he had tried to face it, Moses 'was satisfied'—and so was God.

'Stop thinking like children. In regard to evil be infants, but in your thinking be adults.'

(1 Corinthians 14:20)

Day 36   Leviticus 11:1–12
Your dinner matters to God

We turn now from the tabernacle to the dinner table. Before we dismiss the Levitical food laws as little more than primitive superstition which it would be absurd to try to enforce, or even to draw any lessons from, in the twenty-first century, we must remember this is part of God's revelation and 'everything that was written in the past was written to teach us' (Romans 15:4), and, 'All Scripture is God-breathed and is useful for teaching, rebuking, correcting and training in righteousness, so that the servant of God may be thoroughly equipped for every good work' (2 Timothy 3:16–17).

How then do we respond to these detailed laws governing clean and unclean animals, fish, birds and insects—those permitted for food and those prohibited? Up to this point all the regulations have been concerned with the direct relationship between God and his people. The sacrifices and offerings are all to do with their worship; they governed the welfare of their soul, individually and as a nation. We can understand this language and the symbols because it is spiritual and that is the most important part of life.

However, as the faithful Jew walked away from the tabernacle well satisfied that, having offered a sacrifice with a true heart, he was now right with God, it was as if the Lord arrested his attention: 'Wait a moment, I have something to say about your dinner as well.' What has that to do with God?

God was concerned for the whole person, and he now sets out legislation for the whole life of his people. Over the next few days we will draw out some of the lessons to be learnt from this chapter; in doing so, we discover that no area of our Christian life, not even our food, is outside of God's interest for us. In today's reading, we need not trouble ourselves about the reasons why God warned against certain animals and fish, it is sufficient to notice that he did. The most important question in all the clean and unclean lists that follow is not 'What do they mean?' but 'Who gave them?' God's commands always have a reason, and even when we do not understand the reason, we are expected to obey them. That is all part of living by obedient faith. This need not cause you to eye today's lunch with unusual suspicion, but it may encourage you to say grace with unusual gratitude.

'Whether you eat or drink or whatever you do, do it all for the glory of God.'

(1 Corinthians 10:31)

Day 37   Leviticus 11:13–23

A healthy diet

The true Christian religion is not only a matter of the soul, it governs every detail of life. God is concerned with our food as well as our forgiveness.

Four classes of living creature are involved in this chapter: animals, fish, birds and insects. Small rodents and reptiles are added in verses 29–30. As far as the animals are concerned, those that chew the cud and have cloven hoofs are permitted; a fairly comprehensive list is found in Deuteronomy 14:4–5. Here in Leviticus the negative list is given. Regarding fish, scales and fins are a test for permitted food; shellfish are forbidden. Birds are generally distinguished by whether or not they are birds of prey and carrion. Permitted insects are virtually limited to the locust and grasshopper family.

These are not necessarily accurate scientific descriptions and classifications; for example, the bat may be a 'winged creature' but it is certainly not a 'bird'. However, the LORD's intention is to provide his people with a simple field guide to distinguish clean from unclean. To prohibit the order of *Accipitridae* whilst permitting the *Columbiformes* would hardly be of value to the Israelite boy hurling his sling stone at tomorrow's lunch, but he certainly knew the difference between a vulture and a pigeon!

Before these lists are dismissed as arbitrary and primitive, consider three points of fact:

First, there is universal agreement that, in general, these lists describe that which we do eat and that which we don't. The animals most normally used for food are those that chew the cud (vegetarian) and are cloven hoofed. There are exceptions, but that is an accurate general rule. More people eat lambs than leopards, and more eat bullocks than bears. Similarly, most nations reject the meat of birds of prey and birds that feed on rotting carcases, like vultures and ravens.

Second, it is proven that animals can pass certain diseases to humans both when they are alive and through their meat. It is well known that the more unclean an animal's feeding habits are, the more dangerous its meat may be to humans. All the permitted animals are vegetarians; shellfish are dangerous unless carefully prepared.

Thirdly, God ordained for food those animals that it is most easy to 'domesticate'. It is easier and cheaper to keep a flock of sheep than a pride of lions.

God commands nothing without good reason. He cares for the whole welfare of his people, and in doing so set standards of food hygiene millennia before humanity caught up.

'"Surely this great nation is a wise and understanding people." … What other nation is so great as to have such righteous decrees and laws as this body of laws I am setting before you today?'

(Deuteronomy 4:5–8)

Day 38 Leviticus 11:24–28
Touch nothing unclean

There are literally scores of 'zoonotic' diseases and viruses that are known to transfer from animals to humans, including rabies, psittacosis, salmonella, glanders, MRSA, hepatitis and anthrax. Some are even labelled as 'bioterrorism diseases'! The Israelite knew none of this—but God did. Many of these can be transferred through the blood, which was another reason for the ban on blood and why an Israelite touching an animal carcase mush wash afterwards.

The unpleasant disease of Glanders is passed to humans by horses, and dairymen pick up Undulant Fever from their stock. The terrible bubonic plague (The Black Death) that swept from China to Europe and killed from a third to one half of the population in England in 1348–9, was carried by the rat flea. As long ago as 1885, Dr Noel de Mussy, speaking to the Paris Academy of Medicine, admitted that Moses 'excludes from Hebrew dietary, animals particularly liable to parasites.'

More than three thousand years before modern veterinary medicine, God warned his people about the dangers from infected animals. The carcases of unclean animals were to be treated with particular caution because the disease that killed them may easily be transferred to humans. Anyone, who of necessity touched such a carcase, was to wash carefully and avoid contact with a crowd for the remainder of the day.

We have no need to search for some hidden spiritual meaning here. The law of basic hygiene is obvious to us, but even two centuries ago people were largely ignorant of the dangers of contagious diseases in animals or aware of bacterial infection. These Levitical laws are marks of God's love and care for his chosen people. The surrounding nations knew little of this. True, other nations in the Ancient Near East had food laws, but often they were contradictory or with little meaning; some food could be eaten only on particular days.

The parent who insists on the child washing their hands before commencing a meal is not guilty of a psychotic power mentality or a niggardly demand for primitive taboos. On the contrary, that parent, in the strict enforcement of hygiene, is demonstrating a love and care for the child. So it was with God. It has taken humanity centuries to catch up with the reason for the wisdom of Leviticus.

'No discipline seems pleasant at the time, but painful. Later on, however, it produces a harvest of righteousness and peace for those who have been trained by it.'

(Hebrews 12:11)

Day 39   Leviticus 11:29–38
Lizards and clay pots

In 1751 Captain John Newton complained that he had so many rats on board that they destroyed the spare sails faster than his men could repair them, nibbled at the feet of the sleeping sailors and left their droppings over everything. There was little that John Newton could do because the rodents were part of the community on his small, floating island. Besides, he did not appreciate the full health hazard of those rats and their droppings; on some vessels rat-catchers sold their captives to the crew who cooked and ate them! The only good thing about a shipwreck was the fact that a colony of rats went down as well.

When God presented regulations for the hygiene of his people, he covered even the cooking utensils that might be contaminated. What appears elementary to us has not always been so, and neither is it elementary to many parts of the world today. Wycliffe Bible Translators frequently produce primary reading books containing simple rules of basic hygiene. The rule here to smash the clay cooking pot discovered with a dead lizard in it may seem unnecessary, but it made a significant point, and a housewife would soon learn to leave bowls upside down to avoid having to break them in the morning.

It may be suggested that such laws are not peculiar to the Jews. Before Moses, the ancient Egyptians issued lists of prohibited food. However, if Moses who was instructed in all the wisdom of the Egyptians (Acts 7:22) had merely copied their lists, the book of Leviticus would be very different from what it is. For the Egyptians, the dead were sacred, not unclean; and their regulations were full of absurd instructions; food prohibitions were always based on religious grounds, never hygiene. What mattered was whether this animal was supposedly created by a good god or a bad god. Moses knew all the Egyptian regulations, but he never included them in his instructions to Israel.

It is evidence of the God-given authority of Moses' instructions that nowhere are the foolish potions of men to be found. In 1731 the *Book of Receipts* (recipes) recommended 'snail water'—a concoction of roasted garden snails with a mixture of herbs, nutmeg, liquorice, eggs and milk—to cure 'consumption' (tuberculosis).

Significantly, the revelation to Moses is concerned more with prevention than cure. And that is a relatively modern branch of medicine.

'The foolishness of God is wiser than human wisdom.'
(1 Corinthians 1:25)

Day 40　　　　　　　　　　Leviticus 11:39–45
Eat healthy, eat holy

Much of this chapter is a basic list of hygiene, but it is in the context of God reminding his people that they are to observe these regulations because they are a holy people, and he is a holy God. In other words, even their hygiene is based upon their redemption.

We have referred to various diseases and the danger of bacterial infection from animals; according to scientists in the USA six out of ten known infectious diseases can come from animals. However, God did not approach the subject in this way. The missionary linguists that we considered yesterday tell us that it is often quite inappropriate to say why hands and bowls must be washed; it is impossible for some less advanced people to understand the relationship between dirt and disease; in Europe we have only slowly begun to understand this during the last three hundred years.

God did not instruct his people in the science of bacterial disease, virus infection and preventive medicine; instead, he gave them regulations to prevent bacterial disease and virus infection and said simply: 'If you listen carefully to the LORD your God and do what is right in his eyes, if you pay attention to his commands and keep all his decrees, I will not bring on you any of the diseases I brought on the Egyptians, for I am the LORD, who heals you' (Exodus 15:26). In this way hygiene became a matter of religion.

If we persistently do that which we should avoid because it is clearly injurious to our health or to that of others, that is sin. However, twenty-eight times in this chapter the word 'unclean' occurs; but the word 'sin' does not appear once. Although a lack of hygiene brought a ceremonial uncleanness, this was not sin; but a failure to act according to the regulations in order to make oneself clean was a breach of God's command, and that was sin. God does not have to give us reasons for all that he commands, any more than careful parents will be able to explain all their prohibitions to a toddler. Obedience to God's word must not always demand a reason. God gave the Jews Leviticus 11, and three thousand years later we learnt why.

For the first time in Leviticus we read, 'I am the LORD.' From here on it will occur fifty times until 26:45. It is like a double emphasis, a constant reminder: 'I am the unchanging, covenant keeping God, so never forget your part in the covenant'—in everything.

'We take captive every thought to make it obedient to Christ.'
(2 Corinthians 10:5)

Day 41 Leviticus 11:46–47

Then and now?

These two verses are a postscript summary of the previous regulations regarding clean and unclean creatures. Israel is to be different from the nations around them: 'You are to be holy to me because I, the LORD, am holy, and I have set you apart from the nations to be my own' (Leviticus 20:26). However, these are not arbitrary rules; we may not understand them all but we have seen that so many are for sound reasons.

The question remains: How far are any of these regulations binding upon Christians today? In Colossians 2:16 Paul warns against passing rigid judgements upon matters of food and drink. Abstention from various foods can never in itself aid us in spiritual devotion (2:20–23). In Peter's vision at Joppa (Acts 10:9–16) the apostle was expressly commanded by God to eat 'unclean' food, though this was intended simply as a parable for Peter. However, on the basis of this, the Council of Jerusalem (Acts 15:20) demanded of the Gentile converts abstention only from idolatry, immorality, and two details of Jewish law neither of which concerned clean or unclean animals.

From this we may conclude that the details are no longer binding as our lives becomes less precarious than that of the desert nomad and as modern discoveries enable us to control our food and related diseases. However, the principle stands that what we eat is important not only physically, but since 'our bodies are temples of the Holy Spirit' (1 Corinthians 6:19) Christians have an equal duty to care for it as part of their holiness—set apart from the world to serve God.

Writing in the late nineteenth century, Professor Hosmer commented: 'Throughout the entire history of Israel, the wisdom of the ancient lawgivers in these respects has been remarkably shown. In times of pestilence the Jews have suffered far less than others; as regards longevity and general health, they have in every age been noteworthy.' How true that is may be arguable, but during the plague that swept Europe in the Middle Ages, the Jews were so nearly immune to its ravages that they were accused of starting the infection by poisoning the water supply.

Perhaps we have an obligation before God to be more concerned for the large quantities of additives and junk food that we may consume each day! We may be free to live outside some details of Leviticus, but the Christian will never be free to ignore its purpose.

'Offer your bodies as a living sacrifice, holy and pleasing to God—this is your true and proper worship. Do not conform to the pattern of this world but be transformed by the renewing of your mind.'

(Romans 12:1–2)

Day 42   Leviticus 12:1–8

Childbirth

During the nineteenth century Vienna could boast one of the greatest teaching hospitals of its day; even here, in the maternity wards, one out of every six women died from puerperal fever. The statistics were worse in Britian. In 1847 a young Hungarian doctor, Ignaz Semmelweis, guessed that the reason for such a high rate of mortality was due to the fact that doctors and students never troubled to wash either after autopsies upon the dead, or between examinations of the living. He installed handbasins and insisted on handwashing in a chlorine solution; Semmelweis was ridiculed by the profession, but the mortality rate in his wards declined dramatically to one in eighty-four.

The laws in this chapter do not reflect adversely upon women but continue the theme of basic hygiene with a significant spiritual aspect. It is essential that the young mother and child be isolated from possible infection and that any infection she may develop be kept to herself. Only in a modern hospital is it relatively safe for young mothers and babies to be gathered in the same ward. It would also imply a period of rest before the young mother returned to her responsibilities of caring for the home and family. These regulations are one reason why the Jews have always maintained their population level in spite of severe persecution. Even the ceremony of male circumcision (v. 3), which was a sign of God's covenant with Israel from the time of Abraham, is known to be of medical value.

However, there is something symbolically important here. At the end of her isolation, the mother was to bring a burnt offering for an atonement of her sin. While sickness, contamination, or childbirth could never in themselves bring personal moral guilt upon the individual, the Israelite was not allowed to forget that all disease and the pain of childbirth are the result of the Fall. The reason for the double purification time for the birth of a girl to eighty days may therefore be a reminder of the particular judgment upon Eve (Genesis 3:16 and 1 Timothy 2:14). If there had been no sin there would be no suffering. Even in the joy of childbirth we cannot forget the painful effects of sin.

In the new Jerusalem when the true Israel gathers around the Lamb, there will be no pain, or tears, or death, because the former things will have passed away (Revelation 21:4). There will be no regulations for hygiene and no medical centres. It is no bad thing when bad things remind us of the good things.

'He who was seated on the throne said, "I am making everything new!"'

(Revelation 21:5)

Day 43   Leviticus 13:1–23

Infectious skin diseases

In 1873 the Norwegian physician Gerhard Henrik Armauer Hansen identified the specific *Mycobacterium leprae* that distinguishes what we generally think of as 'leprosy' from the many other forms of skin diseases. It is now known as Hansen's Disease.

The Hebrew word (*sara'ath*) means 'a stroke' and the implication is that it is one of the most awful diseases that fell upon mankind as a result of the Fall. The Greek translators of the Old Testament (*Septuagint*, c. 250 BC) used the Greek word *lepra* which simply means 'scaly'. By the time of John Wycliffe's English New Testament of 1388, the word 'leprosy' (Matthew 8:2) was firmly embedded in our Bibles and over the centuries it focused on what we now call Hansen's Disease.

However, the descriptions used here in Leviticus for diagnosis almost certainly include a wide range of skin diseases. This was the conclusion of Dr Stanley Browne who, before his death in 1986, was a Christian medical missionary and a recognised world authority on leprosy. This is generally accepted, and modern translations therefore refer to 'an infectious skin disease'. The Romans and Greeks referred to *elephantiasis graecorum*, because of the appearance of a hard elephant-like skin; even that name covered a multitude of diseases.

It is possible that true Hansen's disease was not present in ancient Palestine or the lands of the Fertile Crescent as early as the time of Moses. Even in the time of Jesus, and the Middle Ages in England, the word *lepra* could refer to many forms of skin and other infections. Certainly, *Mycobacterium leprae* has no known relationship with wood or fabric, so the later sections in Leviticus must refer to a mould, fungus or rot.

Whatever its true diagnosis, 'leprosy' has always been a feared disease involving mutilation of the body, stinking ulcerous sores, separation from society and, unless healed, a slow and miserable death. The natural fear of leprosy that is found among all nations is evidence of a horrifying course. Aaron's fear for Miriam's punishment provides a dreadful description of *sara'ath*:

'Miriam's skin was leprous—it became as white as snow. Aaron turned toward her and saw that she had a defiling skin disease, and he said to Moses, "Please, my lord, I ask you not to hold against us the sin we have so foolishly committed. Do not let her be like a stillborn infant coming from its mother's womb with its flesh half eaten away"' (Numbers 12:10–12).

Whatever the affliction, the Creator is aware and involved.

*'Look on my affliction and my distress
and take away all my sins.'*

(Psalm 25:18)

Day 44 Leviticus 13:24–46

Isolation

Perhaps the most serious commandment given to the person with a skin disease is found in the last two verses of our passage. When the inspection and the seven days of isolation were completed, the sufferer would wait in fear for the priest's verdict. If the conclusion was 'unclean' they must be isolated outside the camp until the infectious disease is healed. They must tear their clothes as a sign of mourning, leave their hair dishevelled, and cry 'Unclean, unclean' if anyone approached.

This, for what may only be a burn, boil, rash, sore or itch?

To what may appear a harsh and vindictive sentence, it was far more merciful than the general approach of either paganism or Pharisaism. Ancient Hindu law encouraged the leper to take his own life and recommended burial alive. By the time of Christ, the Pharisees virtually drove the leper to death; no one was to greet the leper or approach within six feet. One rabbi would not even eat an egg if it was purchased in a street in which a leper could be seen; and another boasted that he threw stones at lepers to keep them away.

The word 'isolate' occurs eight time in this chapter, and nowhere else in God's law. Isolation was essential for public health. Many skin diseases are contagious: impetigo, shingles, cold sores and scabies are a few better-known examples. Prolonged contact in a tight-knit community certainly increases the risk of infection. The Black Death was stemmed when the church of the Middle Ages began to isolate infected towns and villages. Clearly, healing was always possible. A simple rash, however extensive, did not make a sufferer 'unclean' (vv. 12–13). Raw flesh and open sores would indicate something more serious (vv. 9–11).

God never intended his people to close a heart of compassion towards the leper. He did not deny the right to live and to be aided in a progressive or healing disease. Jesus showed his compassion on those suffering from leprosy—Matthew 8:2–3; 10:8; Luke 17:11–19.

It is commonplace to use leprosy as a symbol of sin. This may be appropriate since, like sin, leprosy defiles and disfigures, is very contagious and left unhealed will lead to inevitable death. However, since in his revelation God has never made this connection, perhaps we should be cautious in making the comparison.

'Love is patient, love is kind.'

(1 Corinthians 13:4)

Day 45   Leviticus 13:47–59

Mouldy clothes

Because the same word *sara'ath* is used of materials such as leather or wool, early commentators were confused since there is no known link between skin diseases and issues in fabric. However, we have seen that the word carries a much wider application.

Even our modern society recognises that the mould, damp and general smell of a garment may make it totally unfit for use and it may have to be destroyed. There is a wise health regulation in these verses. We are aware that diseases can be easily transmitted by various fabrics. A note once found in every public library book proves the point: 'A book exposed to a notifiable disease must not be returned to the library.'

In addition to regular washing of hands, during the Covid epidemic of 2020/21 many households regularly wiped down their food packages or parcels that came into the home—and some still do. God was not giving his people exact scientific descriptions but a ready reference to identify those conditions that, in a warm climate, would be most conducive to the transfer of infection or make an item unfit for general use. If nothing else, the wise hearer of this law would go home and devise the best way of avoiding an unnecessary loss of his tent or clothing!

Once more there is a lesson that runs far deeper than this. God's people were to be unlike the surrounding nations and even their clothing must not be unfit for a people set apart for God. Every part of their life should reflect the pure holiness of the God they served. Like human diseases, even the inevitable decay of uncared-for materials is evidence of the ravages of the Fall. There is no area of life or experience that is not spoiled by the destroying influence of sin. Death and decay are an inevitable part of life.

'The creation itself will be liberated from its bondage to decay and brought into the freedom and glory of the children of God.'
(Romans 8:21)

Day 46 Leviticus 14:1–32
The hope of healing

The Centre for Disease Control and Prevention advises hand hygiene as one of the most important ways to prevent infections. God's instructions for the healed patient to shave, bathe and wash their clothes certainly went beyond simply handwashing.

God always left open the possibility of healing. But it could never be left open to the patient to decide when they were better and safe to return to society; that decision belonged to the priest. The priest was not a primitive 'medicine man' but in effect a doctor trained in specific diagnoses. The instructions here may appear detailed and repetitive, but they are not too dissimilar from a doctor today who carefully examines a rash or a mole to determine its cause and course.

Whenever someone was declared clean, the accompanying ceremony contained a mixture of hygienic and religious regulations. The two birds and the two lambs take us back to the atonement for sin. The bird that flew into the wilderness symbolically carried the defilement away from the sight of the community and from God. The blood of the sacrifice sprinkled, representatively, over the whole body would make the person ask:

'But isn't this for sins committed?' The priest could explain that all disease, though not necessarily for personal sins, is the result of the Fall and human rebellion of which we are all guilty. Part of the ceremony was outside the camp and part within.

Therefore, the Israelite brought a sacrifice. He was free from the disease, and in the excitement stood in danger of forgetting the cause of all pain, disease and suffering—and the God who heals. Today a cluster of drugs are effective again true leprosy (dapsone, rifampicin and clofazimine, and many more for various skin diseases). Our danger is to forget the cause of all disease and that God is still the one who enables the body to be healed, however much modern medicine may assist.

'Jesus reached out his hand and touched the man. "I am willing," he said. "Be clean!" Immediately he was cleansed of his leprosy. Then Jesus said to him, "See that you don't tell anyone. But go, show yourself to the priest and offer the gift Moses commanded, as a testimony to them."

(Matthew 8:3–4)

Day 47 — Leviticus 14:33–57

Unhealthy homes

Because there was no evidence that mould could occur in bricks and stone, according to one early Jewish writer it was mentioned in Scripture in order to give more opportunity for legal studies so that the lawyers could procure a divine reward!

However, here *sara'ath* refers to fungus and mould which are indications of insanitary conditions; an unhealthy environment will lead to unhealthy lives. Both are the result of a fallen world in 'bondage to decay' (Romans 8:21). The Israelite who called in the priest to examine the green growth on the wall of his house, must not forget this. Neither should we, even though we retard the process by a damp course and double glazing. There is one day to be a 'glorious liberty' when a corrupt and corrosive world is ended, and God heralds his new creation by dissolving these elements with fire (2 Peter 3:7–10).

The owner of the house must go and tell the priest, 'I have seen something that looks like a defiling mould in my house' (v. 35). When a house had some evidence of damp and mildew in it, the burden of responsibility was laid upon the owner to admit the problem and tell the priest; the same applied to the presence of a skin complaint in the body or mildew in a garment. There must have been a temptation to keep quiet and hope that the problem would go away; it may not be a severe issue and it seems a waste of a good house or coat for such drastic action to be taken.

Once again, God expected his people to be different from the nations. Wherever possible, they must never allow themselves to become accustomed to unhealthy and insanitary conditions either in their bodies or in their possessions. Deteriorating and harmful homes would not impress a pagan world that God's people were different. If possible, they must take remedial action. In his little book *Primitive Physic* (1747–1780) the evangelical founder of Methodism, John Wesley, wisely commented: 'Everyone that would preserve health should be as clean and sweet as possible in their houses, clothes and furniture.' Had he been reading Leviticus?

It is the same with sinful habits. Too often we would rather cover up and excuse rather than confess our contagion to God. When we find ourselves sliding into some destructive habit, we will convince ourselves that we are still master of the problem and have it under control. There is only one effective course: we must take it to our High Priest—and we must take it there immediately before it spreads. He is the one who, by his own sacrifice for sin, can pronounce us clean.

A new layer of plaster will never eradicate deep mould.

'Since everything will be destroyed ... what kind of people ought you to be? You ought to live holy and godly lives as you look forward to the day of God and speed its coming ... In keeping with his promise we are looking forward to a new heaven and a new earth, where righteousness dwells.'

(2 Peter 3:11–13)

Day 48   Leviticus 15:1–18

Bodily discharge in men

Among the curses that David heaped upon Joab and his descendants for the treacherous murder of Abner was that the household of Joab should never be without someone 'who has a running sore or leprosy ...' (2 Samuel 3:29). These two afflictions would appear to be among those most feared by the Israelite. The exact nature of this 'discharge' is hard to define. It may be a symptom of something contagious and the 'spitting' (v. 8) would therefore refer to coughing and sneezing. In the light of the chapter in general and verses 16–18 in particular, some commentators consider that it has to do with the organs of procreation. It is likely intended to cover the result of disease and incontinence as well as natural emission of semen; normal sexual intercourse is referred to in v. 18.

For some readers the subject is strange for God to deal with, and they may find it offensive or embarrassing. But why? It is true that the Christian should treat certain parts of the body with particular discretion and modesty (1 Corinthians 12:23–24), but this is not intended to build taboos of silence. If God has something to say, he will say it; and we should never set up ourselves as more discreet than God. It is because God invests sex and all its proper functions with approval, and because he considers its abuse, in thought or act, to be one of the greatest disasters in someone's life (Matthew 5:28), that he does not spare the subject in our Bible. The abuse is dealt with in chapters 18 and 20.

It is not that a discharge or an emission of semen is sin, but the consequent ceremonial defilement should make us acutely aware that even this area of our life is related to God. Some things that may be perfectly natural in themselves are still not healthy; hence 'ceremonial uncleanness' debarred the Israelite from the tabernacle. We must hold this area of our life in high regard. Its misuse, in any form, is a concern to God.

The emphasis on washing is another example of God's insistence on personal hygiene among his people. All of which was in marked contrast to what we know of the practices of the surrounding nations.

'That you may become blameless and pure, "children of God without fault in a warped and crooked generation".'

(Philippians 2:15)

Day 49 — Leviticus 15:19–33

Women's menstruation

As in childbirth (chapter 12), a woman becomes ceremonially unclean when performing those natural functions for which she was specifically created and over which she has no control—her regular menstrual discharge. The purpose of ceremonial uncleanness did not involve personal guilt. For example, anyone who touched a dead body became 'unclean' even though somebody had to. Ceremonial uncleanness was God's way of instructing his people in matters of great importance both in hygiene and in holiness. The words 'unclean' and 'uncleanness' occur over 160 times in Leviticus. That is a measure of its importance with God.

The woman with an unnatural discharge, like the woman mentioned in Matthew 9:20–22, or even with her regular discharge, was potentially a health hazard. God was also reminding the woman that her regular inconvenience was a direct result of the Fall (Genesis 3:16). This was equally true of her pain in childbearing (chapter 12). This does not make her childbirth or menstrual discharge morally impure, but it does remind her that even these have a spiritual significance.

There is no inhumanity about God's law; the woman was not cast out of her home but rather left out from daily work to rest. It is only the Israelite law that gave significance to her care.

If God is so concerned in his instructions for our intimate life, is there any area of life that is beyond his scrutiny and care? There is none, and who would want to run their own life when the Master Designer can be in control? There should be no secret areas not yet surrendered to the gaze of God. We may overlook them, but God does not.

'Nothing in all creation is hidden from God's sight. Everything is uncovered and laid bare before the eyes of him to whom we must give account.'

(Hebrews 4:13)

Day 50   Leviticus 16:1–5

The Day of Atonement

We are back with Aaron in the tabernacle. This high priest stands in front of the veil that curtains off the Holy of Holies from the Holy Place. In case he rushes into the presence of God he is ordered to stand still and pay attention to more details of ceremony and ritual. However, this time it concerns the great Day of Atonement.

Some commentators consider chapters 11–15 to be out of place because the first verse of chapter 16 links back to chapter 10. But why out of place? The laws of cleanness and uncleanness would leave many Israelites with the impression that in almost everything they did they would find themselves disqualified from the worship and service of God. The laws were so strict and detailed that we might understand the temptation to despair. How appropriate, then, that God should at this point introduce the summit of atonement—the highest and most holy ceremony of all.

The Day of Atonement was a service that could take place only once a year. The high priest advanced behind the elaborately embroidered curtain (Exodus 26:31–35), stepped up to the ark of the covenant, and fixed his eye on the golden atonement cover over the ark (Exodus 25:17–22). On behalf of the nation the high priest came into the holy presence of God. It was a promise from

God that, in spite of all their failures, there is still access to God for those who trust and believe.

Significantly, the details of the Day of Atonement were given 'after the death of the two sons of Aaron who died when they approached the LORD'. It is when we are most aware of sin and its terrible consequences that we are most appreciative of the atonement. That is why God first laid down the details of cleanness and uncleanness. Let the people first see how impossibly holy God's standard is, and then they will see how vitally necessary is God's salvation. God would only reveal his grace when first the people learned to feel their inadequacy.

Notice what the high priest wore. The gorgeous priestly robe (Exodus 28:2–28) was set aside and he was now clothed all in white. A picture of purity? Yes, but also an absence of pageantry. Colourful ceremony and ornate vestments have no place at the heart of true worship. There was no glitter on Golgotha—only the pure holiness of the Son of God who died there.

'Who may ascend the mountain of the LORD? Who may stand in his holy place? The one who has clean hands and a pure heart.'

(Psalm 24:3–4)

Day 51   Leviticus 16:6–14

History, mystery and secrecy

There are three things to notice in this passage: Aaron, Azazel and the Ark. The first is history, the second is mystery and the third hidden in secrecy!

Aaron first offered a sacrifice for himself and his family; we have met this before (see days 8,10 and 25). The priest must offer for his own sins because he too was a sinful man. Salvation therefore could not depend upon Aaron, for he needed saving as much as anyone. Anyone who stakes their eternal welfare upon a church, a creed, a ceremony, a crucifix or a cardinal would have more chance of survival playing Russian roulette.

Azazel is the Hebrew word translated 'scapegoat'; it is a word with no certain meaning, and views of exactly what it referred to are varied. We will see later that the word may be a personal name, but it may also be understood as meaning 'removal' or 'dismissal'. Here is the first use of the word 'scapegoat'. In 1530 and 1534 William Tyndale, the first to translate the Hebrew Old Testament into English, coined the word *scapegoote*, and by the time of the Geneva Bible of 1560 Tyndale's 'scapegoat' was part of our English language.

However, two things are plain: the goat sent away to Azazel was also an atonement (v. 10) and the animal was driven far from the camp of the people of God. All these ceremonies are pictures for Israel. The life of one goat was taken, and the people saw how severely God will deal with sin; the life of the other was driven away, and the people saw how far God removes their sin. As the animal became a speck on the horizon silhouetted by the setting sun, it was a vivid reminder of God's mercy:

'As far as the east is from the west, so far does he remove our transgressions from us' (Psalm 103:12).

'You will again have compassion on us; you will tread our sins underfoot and hurl all our iniquities into the depths of the sea' (Micah 7:19).

'You have put all my sins behind your back' (Isaiah 38:17).

The gospel according to Leviticus

'I will forgive their wickedness and will remember their sins no more' (Jeremiah 31:34).

Does the Christian require any more assurance and comfort than this? The Israelites may not know where the goat was going, but they knew what went with it.

The ark of the covenant (Exodus 25:10–22) was obscured from Aaron's sight by the cloud of incense 'so that he will not die'. Something greater, better and more enduring lay beyond the vision of Aaron.

'The Holy Spirit was showing by this that the way into the Most Holy Place had not yet been disclosed as long as the first tabernacle was still functioning.'

(Hebrews 9:8)

Day 52   Leviticus 16:15–19

Aaron alone

For once the tabernacle was empty (v. 17). Aaron, the high priest, was alone. The Holy Place and the outer court were abandoned; no priests stood by to offer sacrifices, no eager worshipper came with his sheep or goat. An awful silence hung heavily upon the place of sacrifice. Aaron was alone. If he refused to go forward with this day's activity, there was no one to take his place. If he lost courage at the dreadful responsibility that was laid upon him, then the whole nation lived on without this day of atonement and reconciliation. He surely could not forget the sudden fate of his two sons so recently.

Aaron had to be alone. In no other way would God turn the attention of his people to the One of whom the prophets would speak. Christ came alone from heaven; no angel could share his task. Jesus lived and thought alone—far above his disciples and their tiny faith and foolish understanding. He spent time alone in prayer. He agonised alone in the garden and suffered alone on the cross, failed by men—and rejected his Father (Matthew 27:46). If Jesus had not gone forward to the cross, no atonement or reconciliation would have been accomplished and Aaron's symbolic offering would have been like a signpost to Utopia for a weary traveller—a pleasant thought but with no reality. Jesus had to die alone, so Aaron entered the Holy of Holies alone.

'There was no other good enough to pay the price of sin, he only could unlock the gate of heaven and let us in.' Christ was the substitute for the world, but there could never be a substitute for Christ.

When Aaron came out of this holy place he had 'made atonement for himself, his household and the whole community of Israel'. However, Aaron would have to return a year later, and every day the ordinary sacrifices would be offered. But not so Christ.

'Christ came as high priest of the good things that are now already here ... He did not enter by means of the blood of goats and calves; but he entered the Most Holy Place once for all by his own blood, thus obtaining eternal redemption.'

(Hebrews 9:11–12)

Day 53 Leviticus 16:20–28

The scapegoat

Some believe that the word *Azazel* refers to an evil spirit, perhaps even Satan himself, to whom symbolically the sin of Israel is sent. Perhaps, but it was forgiven sin. Satan is seen as perpetually accusing Christians 'before our God, day and night' (Revelation 12:10 and compare the vivid pictures of this in Job 1:9–11; 2:4,5 and Zechariah 3:1). As the Israelites watched the 'scapegoat' led away into the wilderness they were assured that their sins, all of them, were removed 'as far as the east is from the west' (Psalm 103:12), the punishment had been borne (the goat of sacrifice) and the burden of sin had been removed (the goat of escape)—the people were free from any condemnation by God or accusation by Satan. The means and the result of forgiveness are both here.

We saw on Day 51 how vivid is this picture. The scapegoat was sent away to 'a solitary place' (v. 22), a place cut off and isolated where there are no inhabitants or trackways; the goat can never return to the camp of Israel and will perish in the wilderness. Not only to the people, but to Satan also God was saying: 'There goes the sin of my people Israel; the atonement has been made and their sin is removed. There is no further claim upon them.' That is precisely what Golgotha means to Satan now: 'Having disarmed the powers and authorities, he made a public spectacle of them, triumphing over them by the cross' (Colossians 2:15).

It is a scheme of Satan to wound Christians with a burden of guilt over past sins. We must look to Christ, our 'scapegoat' who carries all our sin, shame and punishment. There can never be condemnation for forgiven sins. Satan knows this. Never allow Satan's understanding of atonement to exceed yours! For the

Christian, there must be no 'tinkering around the tombstones of forgiven sin'.

When Aaron came out from the Holy of Holies, he put off his linen garments 'and he is to leave them there' (v. 23). Is this a foreshadow of the deliberate detail by the apostle in John 20:3–7? New life followed the atonement. Aaron then put on his magnificent priestly robes. Both sets of clothing were holy, but one was more holy than the other. The whole tabernacle was holy, but there was a place called the Holy of Holies. This is a spiritual principle. All activities of the Christian should be holy, but worship is more holy than all. All our speech should be holy, but it is especially a holy thing to sing the praise of our Creator and to speak to others of Christ. All days are holy, but God has set aside one in the week as more holy than others.

'He entered the Most Holy Place once for all by his own blood, thus obtaining eternal redemption.'

(Hebrews 9:12)

Day 54　　　　　　　　　　Leviticus 16:29–34

'A lasting ordinance'

Day after day the priests went about the ritual of sacrifice, both for their own sin and the sins of the people. But on the tenth day of the seventh month the nation stopped work and turned its attention to the high priest and the Holy of Holies. Here, just once a year, the high priest entered into the immediate presence of God. God taught his people under the Old Covenant that although sacrifices must be offered daily, a time would come when a sufficient sacrifice would be offered, not daily, nor annually, but 'once for all'.

It has been suggested that as Isaiah 53 was a climax and summary of all the prophets' expectation of the Messiah, so the Day of Atonement was the climax and summary of all the Messianic ceremonies and sacrifices Moses delivered to Israel—'The most consummate flower of the Messianic symbolism.'

The plain white garments of the high priest on this day represented the One who 'had to be made like them, fully human in every way, in order that he might become a merciful and faithful high priest in service to God, and that he might make atonement for the sins of the people ... yet he did not sin' (Hebrews 2:17 and 4:15). When the high priest next appeared before the waiting congregation, now in his brilliant apparel, he most clearly represented the one who 'will appear a second time, not to bear sin, but to bring salvation to those who are waiting for him' (Hebrews 9:28).

For earthly Israel, this closed their most awesome day of the year, and surely their most joyful. They knew that their sin was covered by the goat of the sin offering; in the goat of escape they watched sin removed from the presence of the congregation and from the eyes of God. This was their gospel.

And it is ours also. In the Lord's Supper we celebrate regularly among the congregation all that both the Passover and the Day of Atonement meant and, as often as we will, we remember it privately in our hearts. In this sense it is a 'lasting ordinance' for God's chosen people.

'He has appeared once for all at the culmination of the ages to do away with sin by the sacrifice of himself.'

(Hebrews 9:26)

Day 55   Leviticus 17:1–9
Worship God's way

The Israelite was commanded to bring all his animals for slaughter as an offering to God, even those for food. He was forbidden to make any sacrifice away from the tabernacle. His gratitude for food must always be directed towards God, and his worship must always be according to God's way. This would be relaxed once the people entered the Promised Land and were scattered over many miles; however, even then they must only offer the animal as a memorial 'at the place the LORD your God will choose' (Deuteronomy 12:15–24). The principle remained: God's way of worship must be followed.

The laws of cleanliness that we have seen were meant to keep the people separate from the surrounding nations. How much more the laws concerning their worship. God was always concerned that his chosen people did not drift back into imitating the world in worship and morality. Israel had been familiar with 'goat idols' in Egypt. Later, the Greeks referred to Pan and the Romans to Faun; each was represented by a creature part human and part goat. It was often accompanied by sexual rituals. Israel must not conform to the society they have left behind or will meet in Canaan.

Here is a principle so needed today. 'You are the salt of the earth. But if the salt loses its saltiness, how can it be made salty again? It is no longer good for anything... You are the light of the world ... let your light shine before others, that they may see your good deeds and glorify your Father in heaven (Matthew 5:13–16). 'Do not conform to the pattern of this world, but be transformed by the renewing of your mind. Then you will be able to test and approve what God's will is—his good, pleasing and perfect will' (Romans 12:2).

It is not for us to worship as we will or to tidy up the Christian faith according to our own preferences or society's insistence. God expects obedience to his word in every area of life.

'Just as he who called you is holy, so be holy in all you do; for it is written: "Be holy, because I am holy."'

(1 Peter 1:15–16)

Day 56 — Leviticus 17:10–16

The ban on blood

God's prohibition against eating blood was not intended to deny blood transfusions or black pudding for the modern Christian! Throughout their long history the Jews learned never to eat blood because there was something especially significant in the blood of sacrifice. 'Shedding blood' describes violent death. This prohibition was reinforced in Deuteronomy 12:23–25.

The ban on blood was not new; it reaches back at least to the time of Noah (Genesis 9:4), although no deeper significance is given there beyond a violent death. Now we learn that since life is represented by the blood, all blood shed, whether in sacrifice or not, is a reminder that the blood of sacrifice 'makes atonement' (v. 11). For Israel, unlike any of the nations, blood had a deep significance far beyond that of the sacrificial animal—it pointed forward to the blood shed when the life of God's Messiah was slain as the ultimate and final sacrifice.

'The law requires that nearly everything be cleansed with blood, and without the shedding of blood there is no forgiveness ... so Christ was sacrificed once to take away the sins of many; and he will appear a second time, not to bear sin, but to bring salvation to those who are waiting for him' (Hebrews 9:22–28).

Although, in deference to the tender conscience of converted Jews, the early Gentile Christians were forbidden by the apostles to eat blood (Acts 15:19,20), this was later relaxed, so long as pastoral care was maintained (1 Corinthians 10:23–33). Today, since blood was part of the ceremonial law all of which has been superseded by Jesus, the Christian is no longer under this restriction. Jesus has broken down the barrier between Jew and Gentile 'by setting aside in his flesh the law with its commands and regulations. His purpose was to create in himself one new humanity out of the two, thus making peace' (Ephesians 2:14–15).

The Ephesian elders were encouraged: 'Be shepherds of the church of God, which he bought with his own blood' (Acts 20:28). Peter wrote of 'the precious blood of Christ, a lamb without blemish or defect' (1 Peter 1:19).

Offensive though it is to the world, a hallmark of the true good news has been an emphasis upon the blood of Christ. Nothing can better portray the fulfilment of all the Old Testament sacrifices. All sin that has ever been or will ever be forgiven is forgiven by the blood of Christ.

'How much more, then, will the blood of Christ, who through the eternal Spirit offered himself unblemished to God, cleanse our consciences from acts that lead to death, so that we may serve the living God!'

(Hebrews 9:14)

Day 57　　　　　　　　　　Leviticus 18:1–18

Unlawful relations

At the end of the *Book of Common Prayer* there are two lists. One list consists of the Articles of Religion, the great body of Christian doctrines that once (but sadly no longer) represented what the Church of England stood for. The other list is quaintly called 'A Table of Kindred and Affinity' and subtitled: 'Wherein whosoever are related are forbidden in Scripture and our Laws to marry together.' There follows a list of thirty female relatives that a man may not marry and thirty male relatives that a woman may not marry. Today, this list is generally accepted in civilised societies as a healthy norm, and much of it is written into the laws of the land. Leviticus 18 is where it originated.

God commanded his people: 'You must not do as they do in Egypt, where you used to live, and you must not do as they do in the land of Canaan, where I am bringing you. Do not follow their practices' (18:3). In Egypt and Canaan inter-family marriage, including incest, was common at all levels of society but especially royalty. It is considered likely this was the cause of the weakness and early death of the teenage pharaoh Tutankhamun. Later, the Greek and Roman gods are witness to a style that prostituted all decency within the family. God had a better way for his people and for what we now know are also reasons of national health.

It is a genetic fact that inbreeding in a closely knit community compounds the poor and weak genes that we all possess and produces abnormalities. Tutankhamun's mummy has revealed he suffered from clubfoot and bone necrosis which left him crippled. When first cousins marry there is twice as much risk of abnormality in the offspring than in other marriages; if such parents have a second child there is a one in four chance of serious defect. The results of such intermarrying are found universally. For centuries members of Europe's royal families often married their close relatives which led to ill health and a higher rate of infant and child mortality. Research has shown that how close they inbred governed their health, intelligence and the success of their reign!

God provided regulations for prevention rather than cure. These regulations of Leviticus are some three thousand years ahead of modern science.

'Oh, the depth of the riches of the wisdom and knowledge of God! How unsearchable his judgments, and his paths beyond tracing out!'

(Romans 11:33)

Day 58   Leviticus 18:19–30
Sexual perversions

God's gift of sexual love in marriage is good and holy in God's sight—the abuse of it is a disgrace. Which is why God condemns adultery, homosexuality, bestiality and cross-dressing as deviations of sexual fulfilment (Leviticus 18:22; 20:13; Deuteronomy 22:5; Romans 1:25–26; 1 Corinthians 6:9 and 1 Timothy 1:10).

Some acts offend against the laws of decency whilst others offend against the laws of humanity. Here God makes no distinction. It is not for us to quarrel with God for placing adultery, infanticide and sodomy in the same passage as the unclean act of v. 19. All represent a lack of self-control and a selfish disregard for the welfare of others. Quite deliberately here and everywhere God jumbles up what society tries to distinguish. All deviation from the high and holy standards of our God are here called 'defilement', 'profanity', 'detestable' and 'perverse'.

An open danger facing Christians today is to trim standards to catch the popular wind of the world. In 1866 Lord Penzance set out the definition of marriage, held for centuries in England, as 'The union of one woman with one man voluntarily entered into for life to the exclusion of all others.' Nearly one hundred and sixty years later, six leading bishops of the Church of England have decided to change this definition of marriage in order to affirm homosexual (gay) marriage. They claimed this change was to avoid 'a radical dislocation between the Church of England and the culture and society we are attempting to serve'. Unquestionably, their standards of morality had been moulded by society rather than God's revelation.

What God wanted his people to avoid here in Leviticus was a slide into the morality of the society around them. Clearly God wanted a 'radical dislocation' between the culture of an unbelieving world and those who truly love and obey him. This is precisely what Jesus and the New Testament letters expected.

The offering of infants in sacrifice to the gods, of whom Moloch was chief, was tragically widespread in the ancient world and, almost unbelievingly, at its lowest point Israel joined in (Jeremiah 7:30–31). God returns to this ruthless ceremony in chapter 20.

Listen to the strong plea of a holy God echoing down the corridors of history: 'Do not follow any of the detestable customs that were practised before you came and do not defile yourselves with them. I am the LORD your God' (v. 30). We may catalogue sins, but should never categorise them; they all belong under the same dreadful headings of 'defilement, profanity, detestable and perverse'. Tread carefully today. You have to walk through Canaan, but 'not as those who live in the land'.

'You adulterous people, don't you know that friendship with the world means enmity against God? Therefore, anyone who chooses to be a friend of the world becomes an enemy of God. Or do you think Scripture says without reason that he jealously longs for the spirit he has caused to dwell in us?'

(James 4:4–5)

Day 59 Leviticus 19:1–8

Various laws

This chapter, like the last, does not offer a complete list of prohibitions, but a sample of the type of life expected of the people belonging to God. It is no accident that here the Lord drew particular attention to the fifth, fourth and second commandments of the Law given on Sinai. Obedience to parental authority is essential since it is well known that a stable family is the bedrock of a stable society.

Obedience to the law of the Sabbath was always a spiritual barometer of the people of God and it still is. Whenever a 'liberated' Christian shakes themselves free from the 'shackles of the law', the fourth commandment is frequently the first rivet to fly. But it is the second commandment that touches close to the character of God, for whenever we set our minds upon things of the earth (Colossians 3:2) we worship the creature rather than the Creator (Romans 1:25) and that is idolatry.

The Israelite was tempted to economise on his sacrifices by making the meat last as long as possible! It was not merely the danger of rancid meat in a warm climate, but the danger of believing that the blessings of yesterday are good enough for today and tomorrow. Christians can fall for the same error. One good quiet time, one strong and effective sermon, one season of spirit-filled prayer, one uplifting conference, and many Christians consider themselves well set-up for a while to come. But this week's wages are not intended to last a month; today's dinner is not sufficient for tomorrow and the next day; and this moment's breath will not last me an hour.

We must never economise on our relationship with Christ but rather capitalise on it. We must seek him each day and learn to walk moment by moment with him. It is true that Elijah travelled for forty days in the strength of one meal, but that is not God's norm. The pattern is spiritual food for each day.

The seventeenth-century minister, Thomas Blake, captured the value of a fresh daily sacrifice of worship: 'Every morning lean your arms awhile upon the windowsill of heaven and gaze upon the Lord. Then with the vision in your heart, turn strong to meet your day.'

'Our Father in heaven ... Give us today our daily bread.'
(Matthew 6:9,11)

Day 60   Leviticus 19:9–25

'I am the LORD'

God has much to say about the Israelite's use of the land, not only because it was an agricultural community but because he is the owner of every acre. He still is. When God urged his people to care for the poor, resist the temptation to dishonest gain and to hand over the first full harvest to him, it is our responsibility to apply these principles today. The changing conditions of life with the passing centuries may have released us from the letter of some of these laws (such as the last two injunctions of v. 19), but we are not released from the principles that led to them.

Not an area of life remains untouched by the God of absolute holiness. Here are compassion, justice, honesty, harmony and purity beyond the highest ideals of the surrounding pagan priests. What is the foundation, the bedrock of all this? Fourteen times in this chapter the phrase 'I am the LORD' is inserted as a serious reminder of the reason behind all our holiness. We are a holy people not because it is nice to be so or safe to be so, but because God himself is.

Holiness and right living for a society must have a yardstick by which it can be measured; a plumb-line by which the uprightness of uprightness may be tested. Otherwise, everyone becomes a law to themselves.

It is strange how much moralising there is in our nation today. The media is quick to condemn celebrities in politics, sport or business, and obviously enjoys doing so. Yet how can a people who have rejected the divine yardstick have any rational ground for condemning others? No one will allow me to measure a length of timber by metres and sell it as 'near enough' so many feet. The only certain guide in life is the holy character of God revealed in his word.

Why is there an absolute rule and authority? Because 'I am the LORD'. How can there be holiness and purity? Because 'I am the LORD'. God, seen and known in the person of his Son Jesus Christ, is the measure of right and wrong. Atheism has no firm ground for a 'rule of law'.

'Just as he who called you is holy, so be holy in all you do; for it is written: "Be holy, because I am holy."'

(1 Peter 1:15–16)

Day 61   Leviticus 19:26–37

Holiness everywhere

Running through all the legislation of God to his people is the theme that they are to be different from the people around them. Once more notice how God deliberately jumbles what we would distinguish. We would hardly place sex slavery (v. 29) in the same category as disrespect for the elderly (v. 32). So why does God do just this? In order to underline that although we may categorise and grade sins, he does not. Sin is sin, whether large or small. In the eyes of God sins that are 'primitive' and sins that are 'civilised' are all sin. Care for the asylum seeker and honest business practices are equally significant to God.

However, it is also true that some sins are more cruel or harmful than others. Satan has a kingdom of his own and part of it is visible and part is invisible. God frequently warned his people against 'divinations, sorcery, mediums, spiritists'. See also

Deuteronomy 18:9–13. The deeper darkness of the occult may not be so widespread in some societies, but the lucky necklace or bracelet, the fairground palmist, the gipsy with her bunch of white heather, the secretive Ouija board or the plain superstition of the average person, all these are much closer to our lives. God warns his people never, even out of idle curiosity, to entertain such evil practices. We should learn from the bitter experience of Saul in 1 Samuel 28. The witch at Endor brought nothing but misery:

'Oh, the road to Endor is the oldest road.
And the craziest road of all.
Straight it runs to the witch's abode,
As it did in the days of Saul.
And nothing has changed of the sorrow in store
For such as go down on the road to Endor.'

Rudyard Kipling was so tragically right. Today millions live under fear, misery and mental distress because they once played with that which God had long ago forbidden. The current rise in this forbidden territory is underscored by the University of Exeter in England offering a master's degree in magic and occult science.

'Many of those who believed now came and openly confessed what they had done. A number who had practised sorcery brought their scrolls together and burned them publicly ... In this way the word of the Lord spread widely and grew in power.'

(Acts 19:18–20)

Day 62 — Leviticus 20:1–9

Infanticide

If there is any crime which violates every mark of decency in human nature it must surely be that of infanticide—murdering children. The king of Moab sacrificed his son in front of the encircling armies of Judah, Israel and Edom and they were so appalled that they withdrew from him and returned home (2 Kings 3:27). Even Ahaz, a king in Judah, 'sacrificed his son in the fire' (2 Kings 16:3), and over a century later the prophet Jeremiah condemned the continuing practice (7:30–31). The Syrians, Phoenicians, Cretans, and many other nations offered the callous pagan sacrifice of children.

The Greek historian Diodorus Siculus, who died in 30 BC, refers to the practice at the siege of Carthage in 310 BC; child sacrifice continued in ancient Rome until outlawed by the Senate in 97 BC. However, and significantly, Tertullian, the church leader at Carthage as late as AD 197 wrote: 'Children were openly sacrificed in Africa to Saturn as lately as the proconsulship of Tiberius [c. AD 14] … And even now that sacred crime still continues to be done in secret'. Tertullian expressed the Christian opposition to all forms of infant and child murder by adding:

'We may not destroy even the foetus in the womb … nor does it matter whether you take away a life that is born, or destroy one that is coming to the birth … It is child murder' (*Apologeticus* IX).

Infanticide is nothing less than counting the unborn child of no value—cancelling its life for the selfish whim of its parents.

The Jewish attitude to children was so unlike that of the surrounding nations, and Deuteronomy 6 reveals this. Firm yet loving discipline and education was the hallmark of Judaism; and it is the hallmark of Christianity. But has a society that neglects the spiritual needs of its children, perverts the books and films that they see, distorts the purity of marriage and gender, and sets an example of pornography and violence by the parental generation, any right to condemn the heinous crime of infanticide? The millions of parents who allow their children to run wild and who, by their own lifestyle, encourage them to scorn that which is pure and holy, and who throw God into the attic with granny's Bible, have all quite deliberately sacrificed their children to the god Molech.

Jewish fathers used to say: 'He who teaches a child is like one who writes with ink on clean paper.' There is some truth in this. However, every adult in society helps to write impressions on the life of our children—for good or bad.

'If anyone causes one of these little ones—those who believe in me— to stumble, it would be better for them to have a large millstone hung around their neck and to be drowned in the depths of the sea.'
(Matthew 18:6)

Day 63 Leviticus 20:10–27

Perversions again

In chapter 18 we saw God's 'Table of Kindred and Affinity' was for the purpose of avoiding the harmful effects of inbreeding in a closed community; that was a biological necessity. Later, in the same chapter, God gave strong warnings against perversions in sexual relations. So fundamental is this to all societies that the

Creator returned to the theme here. Much is repeated because sexual perversions characterise all societies. The further they drift from the spiritual holiness and moral purity demanded by God, the more applauding they are of sexual perversion in every realm.

Whilst it is clearly wrong to commit a sexual union with a married relative, these verses go beyond. There are some unions that are unnatural, indecent and a perversion of humanity created in the image of God. They are described as 'detestable'. Here God places some of the many detestable relationships—including adultery, oedipus lust, sodomy, bestiality and incest—all in the same category.

Reformation of the criminal is not in view in this chapter, but vindication of God's law is. That is the foremost aspect of punishment. An important and holy law can only be seen to be so if it is vindicated. God was insistent: 'You must not live according to the customs of the nations ... because they did all these things, I abhorred them ... I am the LORD your God, who has set you apart from the nations' (vv. 23–24).

We may be tempted to consider the punishment of death for these sins too harsh: has not the gospel of Christ ushered in a new dispensation of grace even for the unbeliever? Today, few would consider it consistent with a Christian view that anyone should be put to death for cursing their parents or even for homosexuality. However, here God reveals what his attitude will always be toward such sins. The judgment on Ananias and Sapphira in Acts 6 may have been unique, but it was not extreme; it warned the infant churches of God's relentless hatred of lies and deceit. Punishments will vary among cultures and across centuries, but God's ultimate judgment never does.

Those who commit these sins in life will always be judged in death. However, there is forgiveness now, for all and any sin—

however great it may be. So holy is God, that to forgive a violation of his law required nothing less than the death of his own Son.

'Since we are receiving a kingdom that cannot be shaken, let us be thankful, and so worship God acceptably with reverence and awe, for our God is a consuming fire.'

(Hebrews 12:28–29)

Day 64   Leviticus 21:1–15

Holy leaders

Some things are holy and some are more holy. This was a lesson that Israel had to learn. As a holy nation Israel was represented by a threefold division: the people, the Levitical priests, and the Aaronic priests. This division corresponded to the tabernacle with its outer court where the people gathered, the Holy Place where the Levitical priests served, and the Most Holy Place behind the curtain where only the high priest could enter. The whole nation was 'holy to their God', but the priests, and still more the high priest, were called to a life of greater holiness. If Israel was to be pure then the priests were to be more pure. Particularly in three areas God spoke to his priests: in mourning, in marriage, and in maintaining purity in the home. In each case the laws for the priests were more stringent than those for the people, and the laws for the high priest were more stringent than those for the priests.

The letter may have passed, but not the spirit. One reason why the church has little impact upon modern society is that the lives of Christian people are often not so different from some in the world around. Where there is honesty and purity and morality in the world, the aim of the Christian is not to ape it but exceed it. If the world has anywhere learnt to face bereavement with serenity, the Christian must be seen more able; if the world can love, care, and show compassion, the Christian must be seen to be more so; if the world can have pure, noble and high thoughts, the Christian must be more holy still.

It was not only that the priests and high priests shunned the evil practices of the people, but they took upon themselves more holy and 'unnecessary' standards. When Paul outlined to Timothy and Titus (1 Timothy 3 and Titus 1) the high standards of Christian life and character of an elder, he did not imply that members of the Christian congregation need not concern themselves with these, but that the leaders must aim to excel in all things.

When Christians complain of narrow views and standards and talk much of being 'free' and 'no longer under the law'—beware! They have probably forgotten their high and holy calling. If every believer is 'a priest to his God', we dare not claim the rights without accepting the responsibilities. We must not enjoy the blessings without practising the duties. What more can you do today to show yourself 'holiness to the LORD'?

'I tell you that unless your righteousness surpasses that of the Pharisees and the teachers of the law, you will certainly not enter the kingdom of heaven.'

(Matthew 5:20)

Day 65   Leviticus 21:10–15
Holy, holy leaders

We return to where we closed yesterday. Earlier in the book of Leviticus we learned of the holy calling of the high priest. By his office and the blood of the sacrifice, by his ministry and the call of God, the high priest, a descendant of Aaron, was declared to be holy and pure in the sight of God. But here are specific instructions so that he may be seen to be holy.

This is where standards and regulations are valuable; they form a yardstick for holy living, a plumb-line of Christian conduct. Some Christians speak so much of inward purity and 'entire sanctification' that they neglect the weighty matters of righteous living. It is wholly correct to say to the young Christian: 'These things Christians do, and these they do not do'—providing they are Bible standards and not human preferences or church traditions.

It is the high priest who is particularly in view here, the leader of leaders among the holy nation. It is never an excuse to cover the moral or spiritual failure of a Christian leader by the suggestion that 'they are only human'. That is true, but it is a reason, not an excuse. The church should never be content to accept ministers and missionaries whose awkward personalities, feeble gifts, lazy habits or dubious character betray their high calling. No Christian leader can excuse themselves on the basis of being 'just human' any more than the high priest could dodge the high standards set for him.

Ministers, elders, deacons, teachers and leaders must all live more holy lives and set more holy standards than those who follow their lead. There are many things they will not do which are not wrong, but the not doing is more holy than the doing.

It was reported some years ago that a Police Inspector made it his business each day to check the tyres and road tax of all the vehicles in the police yard; his reason: 'How can we enforce a law we do not rigidly uphold ourselves?'

'Remember your leaders, who spoke the word of God to you. Consider the outcome of their way of life and imitate their faith. Jesus Christ is the same yesterday and today and forever.'
(Hebrews 13:7–8)

Day 66   Leviticus 21:16–24
The effect of the Fall

These verses may appear harsh, but they are not without good reason. They refer only to the priestly family of Aaron and did not exclude any man from the blessings of the covenant, only from the administration of it. There is always room for Mephibosheth to be blessed by the king (2 Samuel 9). Why did God forbid the lame and diseased from acting as priest at the altar? They were not morally unclean but ceremonially unfit for such service because God had a lesson to teach his people through their infirmity. When a descendant of Aaron limped his way through Jerusalem, a pious Jew would surely be asked by his family: 'Why is this man not a priest?'

That man's lameness, as all afflictions and diseases, was a result of the entrance of sin into the world. It is not necessarily for personal sin that we suffer sickness, but for the presence of sin generally. God was teaching his people that disease and disability was never part of his original creation when 'God saw everything that he had made, and behold, it was very good' (Genesis 1:31). Disease came with sin and sin came at the Fall. The lame were visible proof of the ravages of sin and the need for redemption of both soul and body. The priest, as with the sacrifice itself, had to symbolise, as closely as anyone could, the final and perfectly perfect priest and sacrifice in the person of Jesus the Messiah.

The Jew, as now the Christian, would look forward to that day when there will no longer be pain and suffering and tears; when every broken body of the redeemed will be mended and the hurtful effects of sin spoiling God's creation will be wiped out. All sickness in God's people is ultimately for the glory of God (John 11:4). When the results of sin are finally removed we shall see how magnificently holy is our God.

The unbeliever with an incapacitating or incurable infirmity may be tempted to doubt God's love or question whether they have committed some great sin that has led to their suffering. They may even listen to the superficial 'faith healer' who berates them for a lack of faith and the assertion that nothing is so useless as ill health. However, the word of God will assure them that there can be spiritual health in physical sickness; there are lessons learned in pain and sorrow that can never be learned in robust health. In the context of his own suffering, in 2 Corinthians 1:3–9 Paul introduces the word 'comfort' nine times.

'We ourselves, who have the firstfruits of the Spirit, groan inwardly as we wait eagerly for our adoption to sonship, the redemption of our bodies. For in this hope we were saved.'

(Romans 8:23–24)

Day 67 — Leviticus 22:1–9

'When the sun goes down'

'When the sun is down he will be clean.' Here is a wonderful example of God's positives. There will be many things that make the priest or high priest unclean, but he will not be unclean for ever. Whatever the sin, whatever the defilement, whatever the uncleanness, it will not last for ever; there will be an end of it.

This passage is a summary of the many ways already described in Leviticus by which a priest can become unfit to serve. Some things may quite properly render us unfit for the holy service of Christ; we feel ourselves too soul-dirty to witness or worship. 'Everyone ought to examine themselves,' wrote Paul in 1 Corinthians 11:28 (and 2 Corinthians 13:5), because if we don't, God will. It is wise not to rush carelessly into the presence of God. There are times when it is better to stand at a distance and search our soul. Like the priest, we are so easily disqualified for worship.

However, we ought never to stay that way for long: 'When the sun is down, he will be clean' but only if he has 'bathed himself with water'—a picture of ceremonial cleansing before the day closes. The Christian ought to be no different. Paul made a similar emphasis: 'Do not let the sun go down while you are still angry, and do not give the devil a foothold' (Ephesians 4:26–27). But how could the high priest be clean? 'I am the LORD, who makes them holy' (v. 9). The packhorse has only to return to the stable and his burden is removed, and the Christian has only to return to his Saviour for the same end.

Every day there are countless situations that defile the Christian and, by the enticement of the world or the foolishness of our own heart, the joy and peace of the Saviour is driven off. We may stagger to the evening burdened with the defilement of the world and our personal sin; but a little closing of the eyes and a little folding of the hands will never dispel this burden. Sleep removes tiredness but it is no comfort for a heavy conscience. Only the application of the blood of our Redeemer can effectively remove the defilement of sin.

'As evening approached, the disciples came to him.'
(Matthew 14:15)

Day 68   Leviticus 22:10–16
The priest's table

Two centuries ago, the godly pastor Andrew Bonar wrote of the double tithe in v. 14: 'Discovered sins should excite us to be doubly zealous for the future in repairing the Lord's honour.'

The priest's meal table was as holy as the altar because the meat he and his family ate had first been offered by the people as a sin sacrifice. No-one but the priest and his family were allowed to share that meat and the priest must guard against causing an Israelite to stumble. But accidents do happen, and a man may unwittingly do that which is forbidden. When his fault is discovered, he must pay the double tithe as evidence of his godly grief.

We may sin 'by mistake', but it is still offensive to God and defiling to us. Repentance is not something a Christian does once, but something repeated many times; however, it must come from the heart, and if true repentance comes from the heart, it must also be seen in life. The double tithe was an expression of true sorrow. When Paul described the repentance of Corinth, he used action words: 'earnestness', 'eagerness to clear yourselves', 'indignation', 'alarm', 'longing', 'concern', 'readiness to see justice done' (2 Corinthians 7:11). How real is our sorrow over sin? We have learned to shrug at sins God hates, and wink at sins for which Christ died.

The Lord's Table, like the priest's table, is often attended by those who are not made holy by the blood of Christ. If there was more seriousness—holy reverence and godly fear—on the part of the saints, then perhaps there would be more caution on the part of the sinners.

Whenever we discover sin, we must be doubly zealous to remove it immediately and avoid it in the future. Lion cubs grow into strong and ferocious animals.

'Godly sorrow brings repentance that leads to salvation and leaves no regret, but worldly sorrow brings death.'
(2 Corinthians 7:10)

Day 69 Leviticus 22:17–25

The 'freewill offering'

This is addressed not simply to the priests but to 'all the Israelites'. No exceptions. There are some things which we must give to the Lord because we have promised and it is an obligation; this is the 'votive' (vow) offering. There are other things we may give to the Lord out of no obligation; this is the freewill offering.

The votive offering, like all the sacrifices, must be perfect and without blemish. However, there is one exception in the case of the freewill offering where a defect in no way injures the value of the animal (v. 23). The freewill offering was a glad and happy expression of gratitude on the part of the offerer.

All that we give to God, whether it is our Christian obligation and duty or whether it arises from a joyful desire to show God our love and gratitude, becomes a reflection of our heart, an echo of our secret thoughts. We may give our tithe, but reluctantly. We may give our time and skills in Christian service, but always with half a mind on what we could otherwise be doing. We may offer hospitality, yet regretfully count up the cost of the entertainment and inwardly grumble (1 Peter 4:9). We may attend the prayer meeting, whilst begrudging the loss of a fine summer's evening or a favourite programme. We may come to public worship, but late, out of breath, unprepared and casually.

Centuries later, God complained at the slovenly and careless offering of his people:

'"When you bring injured, lame or diseased animals and offer them as sacrifices, should I accept them from your hands?" says the LORD. "Cursed is the cheat who has an acceptable male in his flock and vows to give it, but then sacrifices a blemished animal to the LORD. For I am a great king," says the LORD Almighty, "and my name is to be feared among the nations"' (Malachi 1:13–14).

Whenever we sacrifice yet complain, we have at once forgotten who we are serving and why we are giving. Beyond our obligation to give our time and money, skills and talents to the service of God, a thankful heart will overflow in a 'freewill offering'. Did Christ give himself half-heartedly for you?

'Whatever you do, work at it with all your heart, as working for the Lord, not for human masters.'

(Colossians 3:23)

Day 70   Leviticus 22:26–33

Animal husbandry is holy

I recall once staying on a farm and being kept awake part of the night by the mournful lowing of a cow whose calf had just been removed from her. It happens often on the farms of our country, and when it does, there is always something hurtful and unnatural about the process. Perhaps part of the significance of this restriction was to encourage Israel to act humanely towards their animals, unlike many of the surrounding nations then and now. This was not the last time that God urged his people to act uniquely in their animal husbandry; even the animals were to benefit from the Sabbath day of rest (Exodus 20:10), and, much later, 'The righteous care for the needs of their animals, but the kindest acts of the wicked are cruel' (Proverbs 12:10).

If the calf, lamb or kid was a type of the sacrifice of Christ, then the full seven days pictures a full and complete life. Despite Herod's bitter hatred, the Messiah would not be killed immediately after his birth but only at the right time. Mary's pain and separation would come: 'A sword will pierce your own soul too' (Luke 2:35); but not until her Son had fulfilled his great mission.

Finally, God's seal of Divine authority is affixed at the conclusion of these detailed regulations. In case anyone should dismiss them as irrelevant or despise them as only the words of Moses, God signs with his signature: 'I am the LORD, who makes you holy' and keeps his part of the covenant always. He is the holy God who is jealously concerned for his honour and will have his own people honour him. If they do not, who else will? He brought his people out of Egypt to honour him before the nations.

So it is with us. Disobedience is profanity. God can always say to his people who protest at sacrifice and regulations: 'Look where you were; look what you were. Have I not done much for you?' Look back gratefully, go forward obediently.

'You are the light of the world ... let your light shine before others, that they may see your good deeds and glorify your Father in heaven.'

(Matthew 5:14,16)

Day 71   Leviticus 23:1–14
Sacred assemblies

The number seven is the number of perfection and completeness. In this chapter we have seven feasts, or 'sacred assemblies', set apart for Israel to remember her God. Each feast is also linked with the number seven. We shall look at the first three today.

The Sabbath. Of all the Jewish festivals this was the most frequent, and the most firmly rooted in the unalterable laws of God. It was the first ever festival established by God at creation (Genesis 2:1–3). It took place on the seventh day of each week, and because it ranked among the Ten Commandments it did not pass away at the entrance of the New Covenant in Christ. The purpose of the Sabbath was a day of rest but also to remind God's people of the God of Creation. 'Wherever you live' brings everyone of God's people into this covenant blessing.

The Passover and Unleavened Bread. Of all the Jewish festivals this was the most historic. At the end of the second period of seven days, in the first month of each year (March), the Jews would relate to their families the tumultuous events of Israel's

Exodus from captivity and slavery in Egypt. This feast reminded Israel of the day they became the nation of God's special choice; it visually portrayed redemption from slavery into freedom. The festival of Unleavened Bread was a fitting inclusion as part of the Passover. A little yeast permeates the whole dough and affects all the bread, so Israel had to leave behind all the Egyptian gods and their ceremonies and the culture that went with it. Only a little sin spoils all our lives. For Israel, their Exodus from Egypt meant a completely new start.

Firstfruits. The Jews would bring before God the first sheaf of their harvest and offer it before the Lord as a symbol that the part represents the whole; it was a recognition that all the harvest is from the Lord, for he is the God of provision.

Of all the feasts only one, the weekly Sabbath, remains unalterably fixed by the Law of God. But others have their types in the Christian's experience. The ex-slave ship captain John Newton annually set apart March 21st as a day of humiliation and celebration for his conversion in 1748, and the godly pastor Murray M'Cheyne always used his birthday, May 21st, as a day of prayer.

Some Christians rejoice to give the first of their salary increase, or the produce of their garden, to the Lord; at one time most Christian churches celebrated an annual harvest thanksgiving in gratitude for the Lord's abundant provision.

Any celebration, if it springs from a joyful and willing heart, is good and acceptable to the Lord.

'You also, like living stones, are being built into a spiritual house to be a holy priesthood, offering spiritual sacrifices acceptable to God through Jesus Christ.'

(1 Peter 2:5)

Day 72 Leviticus 23:15–22
A feast of joy and care for the poor

Next in order came the **Feast of Weeks,** or Pentecost as we more familiarly know it from the Greek word for fifty, because the feast fell on the day following the seventh week after Unleavened Bread. This time it is not a sheaf of the early barley harvest that is waved before the Lord, but two loaves of bread made with fine flour as a symbol of the fulfilment of God's abundant provision. Now, yeast becomes a symbol of plenty. When God begins a work, we should look to him for the completion of it; if we trust him at the start, we should praise him at the conclusion.

The feasts, like the sacrifices, pointed forward to a greater fulfilment. Every Sabbath reminds us of the final rest that awaits the people of God in the glory of heaven and in the peace that Christ gives here in a world of confused turmoil.

'There remains, then, a Sabbath-rest for the people of God; for anyone who enters God's rest also rests from their works, just as God did from his. Let us, therefore, make every effort to enter that rest…' (Hebrews 4:9–11).

Each Passover pointed to One who would deliver his elect from the bondage of sin, the slavery of Satan, and the terrifying prospect of the full weight of the wrath of God. Christ is our Passover lamb (1 Corinthians 5:7). Following close upon the Passover the firstfruits were offered, because after his death Christ rose victoriously to become the 'firstfruits of those who have fallen asleep' (1 Corinthians 15:20,23). Seven weeks elapsed and 'When the day of Pentecost came' (Acts 2:1) God poured out his Spirit as the seal that what he had begun he also would complete.

On this Feast of Weeks yet more firstfruits were offered; a kind of firstfruits from the first fruit. Just as the early Christians became the firstfruits of Christ's death and resurrection (James 1:18).

Significantly, as the celebration of an abundant harvest concludes, the poor and those without a permanent home are not to be forgotten (v. 22).

It is not only the sacrifices that picture a glorious fulfilment in Christ, but the feasts also. If forgiveness of sin finds its truest expression in Christ, so does the festivity of the forgiven heart. Judgment ends at Christ and joy begins there. We come to the Cross repentant and go on our way rejoicing. Christian, begin this day with festivity in your heart. Christ puts it there.

'You ... are filled with an inexpressible and glorious joy, for you are receiving the end result of your faith, the salvation of your souls.'
(1 Peter 1:8–9)

Day 73   Leviticus 23:23–32

The Feast of Trumpets

On the first day of the seventh month the **Feast of Trumpets** was held, and nine days later the great feast of the **Day of Atonement** arrived, on September 10th. The details are in chapter 16. The trumpets of the first day were not intended to awaken a slumbering God and remind him of the approaching celebration. On the contrary, they provided a clarion call from God through his priests to Israel that the holy month of Atonement was here. The trumpets were a call from heaven, not a cry of alarm from earth. The double emphasis on 'do no work' on this day of

Atonement was not intended to spoil their pleasure, but to provide time to focus on the significance of this sacrifice above all sacrifices.

That is the way of our God and his gospel. Salvation is the application of the great work of atonement to the soul of a sinner, but how does it come? It is not, as some would have us imagine, by fallen sinners calling upon God and urging him to action, but rather it is God awakening those who are 'dead in transgressions and sins' (Ephesians 2:1). It is God's initiative; it is his trumpet call that quickens a soul to life. The Puritans called it 'prevenient grace'—grace that is given by God to make us willing to respond. Atonement is accomplished, hallelujah! But what can the spiritual corpse do to receive it until the Almighty God blows the trumpet and awakens the mind, conscience, and soul?

When the trumpet sounded all Israel stopped to listen. They knew that God had prepared an atonement. The work was his. All of it. From first to last. He chose the method, he chose the people, and through his priests he blew the trumpets. Pause for a moment and thank God for the day you first heard the trumpet of God resounding through your soul to awaken you from the slumber of death and to invite you to share in the atonement. Then pray for that trumpet to sound in the congregation on Sunday.

The first trumpet from heaven sounded on Sinai to prepare the people for the law (Exodus 19:16–19). The next and final trumpet from heaven will herald the return of Christ in glory.

'Then will appear the sign of the Son of Man in heaven. And then all the peoples of the earth will mourn when they see the Son of Man coming on the clouds of heaven, with power and great glory. And he will send his angels with a loud trumpet call, and they will gather his elect from the four winds, from one end of the heavens to the other.'

(Matthew 24:30–31)

Day 74   Leviticus 23:33–44

A camping holiday

The Feast of Tabernacles, or booths, was the longest and most joyful festival of all; it was also the last of the seven feasts. There was a twofold significance in this festival: to celebrate the final ingathering of the last of the harvest and to remember how Israel left Egypt and lived in tents in the wilderness. On both counts it was a time of praise and gratitude. From this example, the early Pilgrims to North America established Thanksgiving Day in the Fall of the year.

God looked forward to the day when his people would be comfortably settled in the Promised Land, living in houses of brick and stone. There was nothing wrong with such relative security, for God had brought them there, but there was certainly a great danger in it. In the comfort of the Promised Land they could—and did—so easily forget their origins and the brevity of life. Present security and comfort should never be allowed to blind us to reality. Our earthly present condition is never secure. Our spiritual security has not always been so. Go back and recall your origins.

There is no better cure for those who act as though they are immortal than to spend a half hour walking about a graveyard. Each stone bears an inscription to someone who once lived in this temporary tabernacle and represents a story of suffering and grief. Read the inscriptions and see how many had hope for the future. We know that this 'earthly tent we live in' will be destroyed (2 Corinthians 5:1).

When this festival is repeated in Deuteronomy 16:14–15 this was the invitation by God:

'Be joyful at your festival—you, your sons and daughters, your male and female servants, and the Levites, the foreigners, the fatherless and the widows who live in your towns … For the LORD your God will bless you in all your harvest and in all the work of your hands, and your joy will be complete.'

The Feast of Tabernacles does not stay in the temporary residence. This festival is also symbolic of the heavenly ingathering when the final harvest comes and we enter the eternal rest for the people of God. Joy was the keynote here, as it was at the feast of weeks: joy in what God has done both in redemption from Egypt and in provision of a full harvest and secure homes. How rich and bountiful is our God in his giving: 'The LORD is my shepherd, I lack nothing … Taste and see that the LORD is good; blessed is the one who takes refuge in him. Fear the LORD, you his holy people, for those who fear him lack nothing' (Psalms 23:1; 34:8–9).

'Command those who are rich in this present world not to be arrogant nor to put their hope in wealth, which is so uncertain, but to put their hope in God, who richly provides us with everything for our enjoyment.'

(1 Timothy 6:17)

Day 75   Leviticus 24:1–9

Oil and bread

The annual festivals have now been given. We should expect the Sabbath and Jubilee years to follow at once. We are therefore surprised to find this chapter intervening. Many are unable to find an adequate reason why the lampstand and table of 'shewbread' should come at this point. However, if we look at the type of which these ceremonies are only the shadow then the reason is plain. What comes between the Christian's experience of salvation from a past life and the expectation of a final harvest home? Surely it must be commitment and service.

The golden lampstand (later known as the Menorah from the Hebrew word for 'lamp') with its seven lamps (Exodus 25:31–40) remained unexplained for a thousand years until the time of Zechariah when the vision of a lampstand given to Zerubbabel was interpreted: '"Not by might nor by power, but by my Spirit" says the LORD Almighty' (Zechariah 4:6). As the oil represents the Spirit of God, so Israel was always intended to be a light to the surrounding nations. But there is no light without the oil.

When Jesus claimed, 'While I am in the world, I am the light of the world' (John 9:5) he was not suggesting there would be no more light when he had gone. Christian communities across the globe are to be the light of the world (Matthew 5:14), but without the Holy Spirit they will never be what they should be.

It was a perpetual light from the lampstand, and Aaron's task was to see that it was so. Only the constant vigilance of the high priest could ensure the light did not go out. Our great High Priest tends his Church to guard and keep its light pure and bright. If the light of the Church goes out, the whole world will lie in darkness.

The twelve loaves of bread, representing the whole company of God's people 'an offering made to the LORD ... on behalf of the Israelites, as a lasting covenant', was perpetually stocked and renewed each week. It is a picture of the Christian's perpetual consecration to the Lord of all that they are and all that they have; a consecration that is never allowed to grow hard or stale. Pray for a perpetual holy freshness about our love and service for Christ.

'I saw seven golden lampstands, and among the lampstands was someone like a son of man.'

(Revelation 1:12–13)

Day 76   Leviticus 24:10–16
Blasphemy

Together with the ordination of the priests of Aaron and the Levites in chapters 8 and 9, there are only two other historical interludes in Leviticus: the judgment on Nadab and Abihu in chapter 10 and this equally tragic episode.

It is probably more fashionable today to violate the third commandment than any of the other nine. In general, it has become acceptable to reinforce a conversation with 'holy' expletives rather than the more crude and lower forms of language. The Christian heart may shudder at the judgment so many carelessly invite upon themselves. God will hold no one guiltless for the casual: 'O God!', 'my Lord!', 'Christ!', 'Jesus Christ!', 'God knows!' and more.

Tragically, the careless conscience soon ceases to bring any conviction at all. The night before George Müller, whose life of faith and care for orphans is legendary, took his first communion, and long before his conversion, he committed shameful acts of sin, withheld eleven-twelfths of the confirmation fee entrusted to him by his father, and lied his way to the communion table. His biographer concludes: 'Sacred things were treated as common, and so conscience became the more callous.' Similarly, a century earlier, John Newton excelled so greatly in blasphemy that when he ran out of oaths he invented new ones and his godless language appalled even his hard-swearing sea captains.

This is not the first time God raised the subject of blasphemy with his people (Exodus 20:7 and 22:28). To blaspheme God's name is to despise his character. The example of the judgment on the bi-racial young man will vividly show the nation, and us, what God thinks of such a slur on his holy character. The judgment was hardly different fifteen hundred years later when Ananias and Sapphira died for dishonesty (Acts 5).

God has not changed his view of this form of bold, indifferent arrogance. There are few sins that do greater damage to the soul. Is this part of the 'blasphemy against the Spirit' in Matthew 12:31? Let every Christian make a careful inventory of their own expletives. Is there one blasphemy among them? But is our blasphemy any less real when we treat casually holy things? To say 'Amen' to a prayer we have barely listened to, noisily disturb others in worship by a late and clumsy arrival or ceaseless chatter; allow a wandering mind during the sermon or the Bible reading or at the Lord's table? We may trust in the sacrifice of Christ to relieve us of this guilt, but what damage is it doing to our soul?

A leaking hull must be stopped before the ship can go to sea, and if there is a Jonah on board he must be thrown out—or left behind before you sail.

'Holding on to faith and a good conscience, which some have rejected and so have suffered shipwreck with regard to the faith. Among them are Hymenaeus and Alexander, whom I have handed over to Satan to be taught not to blaspheme.'

(1 Timothy 1:19–20)

Day 77   Leviticus 24:17–23

Retribution and restoration

In this passage punishment was to be settled on the principle of *lex talionis*, life for life. In spite of what so many think, this principle is not contradicted by Jesus in Matthew 5:38–39: 'You have heard that it was said, "Eye for eye, and tooth for tooth". But I tell you, do not resist an evil person.' In context, the Jews had taken this passage in Leviticus to give them licence to wreak personal vengeance upon anyone. The judgments listed here were to be pronounced only by the judiciary. The Christian may resort to the law, but never to their own retaliation.

Here both retribution and restitution are in view and governments would do well to consider them. If God allowed it, capital punishment cannot be wrong for contemplated and callous murder. Today our laws of punishment have a misguided response too often. The alarmingly high return of offenders to their prison within a short while after release—in some prisons as high as one third—proves the point. What is better suited in many cases is restitution by the offender, not compensation by a benevolent government. A return to the Bible could be a return to reality and justice.

Vindication is not the same as vindictiveness. There is nothing petty about these laws; they treat human life, limb and property seriously. If anyone violates the laws of the sanctity of life and property, then they must forfeit the right to it. In some cases, restitution is the only way in which many will learn the enormity of their crimes.

It is not so strange that God should close the section, that began with witness and consecration, with punishment for criminal acts. Surely our own evangelistic zeal and our profession of sanctification will mean nothing if we do not hold a high view of human life and property, and a serious view of the violation of them.

'We know that God's judgment against those who do such things is based on truth.'

(Romans 2:2)

Day 78   Leviticus 25:1–7

Fallow land

The seventh year must have been a delight for every child and a frustration for every farmer. During this year there was to be no sowing and no harvesting. The people could eat freely of what grew by itself just as they required a day's food, and the children would be glad of the invitation to 'help themselves'. No harvest was to be reaped, no barns filled, and no seed gathered for sowing. One year in seven the land was left 'fallow' and no cultivation of crops was allowed.

'Fallowing' did not end with the Bible, although it may have started there. The system was widely employed in Britain from the Roman occupation onwards. In my library I had a large volume dated 1860 and entitled simply: *British Agriculture*. A modern textbook of its day, fallowing is recommended as an indispensable part of good land husbandry. Commenting upon the few who despised the system the book concludes: 'These persons only shew their own ignorance and evince a total unacquaintance with the stubborn soils that require that operation. No mode of cultivation yet known can supersede the necessity of that pulverization and cleaning effected by fallowing…'. In agriculture this 'pulverizing' meant allowing the heavy soil to be broken into finer soil by leaving it to rest.

For the good of the land and thus for the good of future crops, God commanded the system of a year's fallow.

As a mark of 'progress', a book also in my library of agriculture in the mid twentieth-century commented on this traditional method of restoring the vitality of hard worked soil: 'Fallowing is looked upon with disfavour today … with the greater powers provided by the tractor, by improved implements, by more varied crops, and by the use of chemicals, we can control weeds; and with the use of artificial fertilisers we can easily supply the additional plant foods that resulted from a fallow.'

However, anyone up to date with modern farming and ecology discussions will know that fallowing and similar 'land resting' approaches are topics keenly debated today. The huge machinery compressing the land and the run off and overuse of those 'chemicals' and 'artificial fertilisers' are the very things many experts conclude are ruining our soil structure and polluting our rivers. Is ecology and the need for more healthy soil turning us back to the Bible?

This programme reminded the Jew of a wide application to his psalm that 'The earth is the LORD's, and everything in it, the world, and all who live in it' (Psalm 24:1). God's command is no arbitrary rule, but a careful and scientific approach to help humanity make the best use of the land he has created. However, it is more. The seventh year of rest for soil and toil was also a picture of the final rest in the new heaven and new earth.

'Then I heard a voice from heaven say, "Write this: Blessed are the dead who die in the Lord from now on." "Yes," says the Spirit, "they will rest from their labour, for their deeds will follow them."'
(Revelation 14:13)

Day 79 — Leviticus 25:8–17

Jubilee!

Here, and in 26:46, we are reminded that these laws were not afterthoughts of Moses; they were given by God when Moses received the law on Mount Sinai (Exodus 31:18).

The fiftieth year followed immediately after the seventh Sabbath fallow year. Two years without a proper seed time or harvest! It was called the Jubilee, and our English word is simply a transliteration of the Hebrew *Yobel* (a word that carries the idea of freedom); it was to be a time of shouting and gladness—a 'joybellee' and with good reason. Leased land reverted to its proper owner, debts were remitted, and Hebrew slaves returned home freely. The only Jews displeased with the whole arrangement would be the large landowners and moneylenders who accumulated vast fortunes of wealth by impoverishing and enslaving fellow Jews.

In the year of Jubilee something of the inequalities were remedied. But let no one take this to support an unsteady political philosophy. If the regulation appears to avoid excessive capitalism, there was plenty of incentive in Israel for private enterprise. Hard and honest work was always well rewarded, while lazy sluggards had nothing at the end of fifty years but that with which they started, and the knowledge that their children would for ever suffer for their slumber.

This chapter contains the earliest system of leasehold known. Our English feudal system gave no security to the tenant farmer, and it took a thousand years to write leasehold laws into our statute books. God gave them to his people more than three thousand years ago! Whenever a man purchased a lease or rented land, or borrowed a loan, he knew exactly for how long the arrangement would stand, and terms were agreed accordingly.

Everything about the Jubilee was designed to overthrow greed and selfishness. 'Do not take advantage of each other' (v. 17), and that is the simple difference between honest and dishonest business, just and unjust transactions. Let every Christian businessman be able to look all his clients or customers in the face and declare: 'I have wronged no one.' It was because God intended his people to respect one another that he expected them to respect one another's property also. Honesty is an attitude towards people before things.

The only other reference to the Jubilee is in Numbers 36:4. Sadly, because the nation neglected this Jubilee privilege, there is no clear record of it ever taking place, and it is one reason why the people were taken into captivity (2 Chronicles 36:21). When the Jubilee was neglected, landowners exploited the common people. Nehemiah may have been reinstating the Jubilee when the people cried to him, 'We have to subject our sons and daughters to slavery. Some of our daughters have already been enslaved, but we are powerless, because our fields and our vineyards belong to others' (Nehemiah 5:5).

'Be kind and compassionate to one another, forgiving each other, just as in Christ God forgave you.'

(Ephesians 4:32)

Day 80　　　　　　　　　　Leviticus 25:18–24

'The land is mine'

An obvious objection is raised: if the people could not sow or reap in the seventh year then how could they harvest in the eighth? There would be famine by the ninth. Israel's fallow year was for the whole land, not merely an odd field or two. It was at this point their faith in God was on trial. God promised that the sixth year would produce sufficient for the seventh and eighth; and here was a situation where God gave the evidence before he called for obedience. The abundant harvest of the sixth year left the people in little doubt as to what must follow.

Every harvest should reaffirm our confidence in God. He is still the God of 'seedtime and harvest, cold and heat, summer and winter, day and night' (Genesis 8:22). When God reminded his people: 'the land is mine', he was making a statement of scientific, as well as theological, fact. We talk of the 'laws of nature', and worse, 'mother nature', as if nature was a fairy god-mother capable of creating vast and intricate laws. In reality, the laws that govern nature are given and upheld by God. Every harvest belongs to God. Ultimately it is God who gives or withholds, and when he withholds the rainfall we can do little more than pray and wait.

The Levitical laws of leasehold and the year of Jubilee were both a strong reminder to Israel that they lived in the land only temporarily and held it upon trust from God. This fact has not changed. All of us walk briefly across the land; we may flourish like spring grass, but soon the sickle cuts us from the earth and we lie dead and withered upon the ground. In our short space and pace of life we are all accountable to the heavenly Landowner for what we do with the small plot entrusted to us. The Christian, like Israel, does not walk alone across the field of life, but as a stranger and pilgrim with God (v. 23). There is no better way to live or die.

'All these people were still living by faith when they died. They did not receive the things promised; they only saw them and welcomed them from a distance, admitting that they were foreigners and

strangers on earth ... They were longing for a better country—a heavenly one. Therefore God is not ashamed to be called their God, for he has prepared a city for them.'

(Hebrews 11:13,16)

Day 81   Leviticus 25:25–28

The 'nearest relative'

God avoided exploitation and perpetual poverty among his own people. The poor always retained the right to redeem that which they were forced to sell; and it would return to them in the year of Jubilee. The image of the Jew as a sharp and ruthless businessman, wizard in finance and a genius in trading with little thought or care for the welfare of others is certainly not a Biblical portrait. Into all their business dealings God built in safeguards against a Merchant of Venice mentality. If God gave gifts of administration of property and finance to his people, he also gave restraints to a ruthless zeal in the exercising of those gifts. This pattern and principle has not changed. Scrupulous respect for others will lead to scrupulous honesty towards them.

More than this. A man's next of kin had an obligation to help his relative in need. The 'nearest relative' (v. 25) is the *goel* or 'kinsman redeemer', and the responsibility of care was a matter of morality and legality. It is beautifully illustrated in the biblical story of Boaz and Ruth.

Today's society has downgraded the value of the family to the point at which family loyalty and support are sometimes regarded as unnecessary burdens. Perhaps it's not new. Faced with a number of destitute widows in the churches, Paul urged the relatives to accept their God-given responsibility: 'If a widow has children or grandchildren, these should learn first of all to put their religion into practice by caring for their own family and so repaying their parents and grandparents, for this is pleasing to God' (1 Timothy 5:4). Apparently, some were not doing so.

We dare not contend for a God-given basis for the family unit and yet ignore its responsibilities. The state may now do much, but it cannot provide the love, peace, or security of belonging to a caring family. At one time grandparents were the patriarchs and matriarchs of the family; they were not merely free baby-sitters for the parents and free sweets for the children, they were the source of wisdom and advice. How much poverty and suffering could be avoided today if families looked after one another? The next of kin are not merely executors of the estate of the deceased.

This kinsman redeemer is illustrated in the Messianic expectation. God provides our kinsman redeemer in his Son. In Isaiah 61, the prophet described the *goel* that God provided for this people; and when Jesus read this passage in the synagogue at Nazareth, he closed the scroll declaring, 'Today this scripture is fulfilled in your hearing' (Luke 4:21). Job longed for this *goel*.

'I know that my redeemer lives, and that in the end he will stand on the earth … in my flesh I will see God; I myself will see him with my own eyes—I, and not another. How my heart yearns within me!'

(Job 19:25–27)

Day 82　　　　　Leviticus 25:29–34

Caring for the Levites

The house belonging to a farmland could never be sold freehold and, unless redeemed beforehand, must always revert to the farm in the Jubilee year. This was because the land was unusable if a dwelling was not close by. On the other hand, city homes had no farmland relying upon them and they could be sold freehold. It was always the land that was important because it belonged to God, and no one was allowed to accrue vast estates.

However, the Levites, those set apart for the service of the tabernacle, were allowed special regulations to govern their property. The design behind these regulations was to ensure that no Levite would be homeless or landless, and thus could be free of anxious care over matters of finance and property. Everywhere God showed himself careful for the practical welfare of those who ministered spiritual welfare. Poverty and spirituality are not cause and effect! The simplest way of keeping a man 'other worldly' in his thinking is to give him no cause to worry about what he will eat, drink or put on, either for himself or for his family.

Apparently, God knew about this more than three thousand years ago, because the Levites were adequately and regularly provided for. Perhaps the Church of Christ has always been slow in coming to terms with God's wisdom. When Nehemiah came to Jerusalem, he discovered the Levites were neglecting their temple duties in order to tend their fields. The reason was that 'The portions assigned to the Levites had not been given to them, and that all the Levites and musicians responsible for the service had gone back to their own fields.' (Nehemiah 13:10).

Nehemiah, afraid of the face of no man, 'confronted the officials.' God still does, and Jesus did: 'for the worker deserves his wages' (Luke 10:7). Church leaders are sometimes slow to hear and even slower to respond. Some churches are glad to put out their minister to tend the fields because it is cheaper that way. Then they wonder why the 'house of God is forsaken'. I have yet to discover a thriving, growing church that is mean and niggardly to those who give themselves wholly to minister the word. When the Levites were forsaken so was the house of God.

'The elders who direct the affairs of the church well are worthy of double honour, especially those whose work is preaching and teaching. For Scripture says, "Do not muzzle an ox while it is treading out the grain," and "The worker deserves his wages."'
(1 Timothy 5:17–18)

Day 83   Leviticus 25:35–46

Interest and slavery

Rather than a cap on interest rates, God placed a wholesale ban! Loans, yes; interest, no. This was unique among the nations around them who sometimes added as much as twenty-five percent. Although Israel could charge foreigners interest, among the Israelites and foreigners who live among them, their holy separation from the surrounding nations would be seen in their generous care for one another. An absence of exploiting the poor would be an example to the nations. In Exodus 22:25–27 and Deuteronomy 23:20 even free loans were carefully guarded against exploitation. The difference between a slave and a hired worker was significant. No Israelite could be a hired worker beyond the year of Jubilee.

Here is a distinction between slavery and the carefully regulated treatment of hired servants (Exodus 21:1–11). Although slavery among the Israelites was forbidden, they were allowed to take slaves from the surrounding nations in times of war; yet still with conditions attached.

Is it strange that God should allow slavery under any circumstances? Even Queen Elizabeth I warned Sir John Hawkins against the trade: 'It would be detestable and call down the vengeance of heaven upon the undertakers.' Despite this, man-stealing, the heart of both the European and North African slave trade from the sixteenth century onwards, flourished. But it had long been condemned by God (Exodus 21:16; Deuteronomy 24:6) and Paul underlined this in 1 Timothy 1:10 where 'slave traders' were listed among some of the worst crimes of humanity.

God allowed many ancient practices: 'Because of the hardness of your heart' (Matthew 19:8). Frequently Christian morality has accepted a less-than-ideal situation—polygamy is one example—and sought only to regulate it from extreme abuse until the people came to a clearer understanding. Paul's treatment of the slave/master relationship was radical in his time (Ephesians 6:5–9). Similarly, nowhere was the slave treated with so many rights or with such care as in Israel.

It would be a shameful thing for Christians to give generously to the needs of society in general and to neglect their own members. We are to 'love one another as Christ loved us'; that is where true Christian love must always begin.

'Do good to all people, especially to those who belong to the family of believers.'

(Galatians 6:10)

Day 84 — Leviticus 25:47–55

Rescued to serve

We conclude a whole chapter where God seems concerned with little else than the nation's business transactions: house and land purchase, leasehold, freehold and mortgaging, money lending, agricultural investment, and the labour market. All are dealt with here, and all have a familiar modern ring about them; we could almost be reading the headlines from today's *Financial Times*.

But why should this be strange to us? We have agreed often through Leviticus that God is concerned for every part of life. The house you are about to purchase, the mortgage you are negotiating, the new job you are investigating or the labour you are recruiting, each has its place in the plan and care of God. Our society is very different from that of Israel fifteen hundred years before Christ came, but some values of business relationships never change. Here God refers to the capital gains that enable even a foreigner to 'become rich', but he also is bound by the laws of God's people.

God is concerned to place a check on the natural tendency of covetousness and greed. In Israel there would be no vast estates owned by wealthy magnates, all at the cost of the miserable poverty of most—which has ever been the story of all societies. Here also is a reminder of the brevity of all our possessions and that God alone is the owner of everything.

The governing principle of all our dealings with others is found in the final verse of this chapter. We are all servants of God and as such have no right to deal harshly or unjustly with others. The employee and employer must deal with one another knowing that 'he who is both their Master and yours is in heaven, and that there is no favouritism with him' (Ephesians 6:9).

All this is set in the context of the covenant relationship between God and his chosen people redeemed from slavery in Egypt. When two men are rescued from the same terrible fate, it is natural for them to feel a close kindred and affinity, however much they may differ socially, culturally, intellectually, academically or financially. It would be unnatural for either of them to exploit the other since both were within a hairs breath of possessing nothing. Our distinctions fall to the ground like a heavy oak plucked up by a tempest when we recognise from what we have been rescued and by whom. When we serve God with gratitude for such a great salvation then we will serve one another and transact all our business accordingly.

'Whatever you do, whether in word or deed, do it all in the name of the Lord Jesus, giving thanks to God the Father through him ... Work at it with all your heart, as working for the Lord, not for human masters, since you know that you will receive an inheritance from the Lord as a reward. It is the Lord Christ you are serving.'
(Colossians 3:17, 23–24)

Day 85 Leviticus 26:1–13
'I will walk among you'

There are sure blessings in obedience. What a glorious array of blooms is found in the garden of those who obey the rules of horticulture; what a splendid and secure building is designed by those who obey the rules of correct architecture. In every sphere of life, from the cradle to the grave, there are blessings in obedience.

With all the promises of regular rainfall, bountiful harvests, unimagined peace and unparalleled security, there was something even greater for the people of God. It is true that there are many earthly blessings for the obedient Christian: God may prosper their business, preserve their health, protect their family and provide much more besides—he may. But we will doubt the reality and sincerity of their faith if this is their major concern. If, like the nine lepers of Luke 17, they come for physical healing and are fully content when that is received, we may well question whether they know anything of real blessing. Surely the heart of God's promises for obedience is found in v. 12: 'I will walk among you and be your God, and you will be my people.'

That is the true and lasting blessing. As God walked with Adam and Eve in the garden in the cool of the evening, so God walks with his chosen people. The greatest blessing Israel ever experienced was not military or economic prosperity—they were merely 'fringe benefits' of obedience—but the presence of the Lord God among them. In the opening of this chapter, God selected three commandments as typical of them all. He chose the first two, which are concerned with our relationship with him, and the fourth. Have you noticed how frequently in Leviticus we return to the fourth commandment?

In Luke 17 only one leper returned to worship Christ, and he was the only one really blessed. Doubtless he went away 'with his head held high'. How often do we receive blessings from Christ, but we do not receive Christ from the blessings? The glorious anticipation of heaven is the continuation of our present relationship with God.

'Jesus replied, "Anyone who loves me will obey my teaching. My Father will love them, and we will come to them and make our home with them."'

(John 14:23)

Day 86　　　　　　　　　　Leviticus 26:14–26
'I will set my face against you'

During the Battle of Waterloo in 1815, the Scots Greys made a magnificent charge into the French lines; they scattered the artillery and silenced many guns. Unfortunately, they were so intoxicated by success that they refused the bugler's recall, and the squadron was virtually destroyed by Napoleon's Lancers. Implicit obedience is as important in victory and success as it is in defeat. Israel would learn throughout her future how much misery and suffering is occasioned by disobedience.

It is a bad law that does not spell out the penalties of contravention. God certainly gave his people the divine declaration of intent in unmistakably clear terms. The subsequent suffering of the Jews, which at times has been tragically severe, must always be viewed in the light of this chapter. A people cannot expect to live in the privileged position of God's elect nation and live as they please. They cannot expect unalloyed blessing and give rusted service in return. The law of God is the clarion note of the bugle recalling the people back to the lines, and if they disobey, then the whole nation will be destroyed. The history of Israel illustrated this only too clearly.

However, the principle has not changed for the Christian. We may bask in the blessings of justification and forgiveness like some great whale unaware that the tide of obedience and sanctification is running out. Too often there are complaints of spiritual barrenness that find fault with the sermons, the behaviour of Christians, our adverse circumstances—anything but ourselves. Perhaps these severe verses would point the finger in the right direction. God will not allow his people to sin without reaping the harvest, any more than he will ultimately allow the world to do so.

If we feel currently under his discipline, God may be saying, 'If you continue to be hostile toward me' then I will be 'hostile toward you' (vv. 23,24). Can you hear the bugle to return to the lines? Then obey its call now, before it is too late.

'My son, do not make light of the Lord's discipline,
　and do not lose heart when he rebukes you,
because the Lord disciplines the one he loves,
　and he chastens everyone he accepts as his son.'

(Hebrews 12:5–6)

Day 87　　　　　　　　　　Leviticus 26:27–39

The tragic story of Israel

Since the Roman legionaries ploughed up Jerusalem in AD 135 until the 'Six Day War' of 1967, the Jewish nation could never fully claim it occupied the Land of Promise. For centuries, Jews wandered as a hated and despised people—a nation without a home. All Jews were expelled from England by Edward I in 1290 and it was not until 1656 they were officially readmitted by Oliver Cromwell; but until 1858 they were denied a seat in Parliament. The picture was the same or worse everywhere, until Israel was proclaimed a nation in 1948. However, it was not until 1967 that the nation could claim to occupy her ancient and rightful land. Even this claim is tenuously maintained and only at enormous military cost to protect them from aggressive neighbours. Even now, the majority of Jews live away from Israel; these are the 'diaspora' or dispersion.

However you may interpret the history of the Jewish people, their story reads the same. They are a unique and amazing people that appear to have been under a singular discipline from God for two thousand years, a discipline tempered only by an ultimate and loving purpose. The terrible suffering of the Jews since their rejection of their Messiah is mirrored all too plainly in this passage; and much of it was fulfilled even before the close of the Old Testament. Here, the warning points on to the years of exile from the defeat of Samaria in the north by the Assyrians in 722 BC to the destruction of Jerusalem in the south by the Babylonians in 586 BC. Thousands died in exile.

God warned his people in bleak and plain language: 'If in spite of this you still do not listen to me but continue to be hostile toward me, then in my anger I will be hostile toward you, and I myself will punish you for your sins seven times over' (vv. 27–28). That is a sad summary of Israel's history.

How much more is it true for an unbelieving world. Much of so-called Christendom is spiritually dead and so many churches are only playing at Christianity. We can never smother disobedience with religious activity (v. 31). God hates that. He does not wink at hypocrisy from wherever it comes. However, this suffering is not God forcing it upon a nation, it is the inevitable result when he withdraws his hand of protection. Here is God's description of what happens when we are left to ourselves:

'Because you are lukewarm—neither hot nor cold—I am about to spit you out of my mouth.'

(Revelation 3:16)

Day 88   Leviticus 26:40–46

'I will remember my covenant'

There is great comfort for those who belong to God. Even under his rod of discipline, even when we are walking contrary to him, God will remember his covenant (v. 42). When twice God refers to his people 'paying' for their sins, this is not a payment for redemption but for our discipline; just as we would warn someone that they will have to pay for their foolish behaviour by its negative outcome. There are blessings for obedience but also sanctions for disobedience.

In these verses we are reminded of the unbreakable covenant provided by the unshakable love and unalterable grace of the immutable God. Once we have been adopted into his family, nothing can change his covenant love towards us.

We may, in the foolishness of a backsliding heart, spurn his kindness and defy his laws (v. 43), but never will he so utterly cast us off that we become as if we had never been saved by the covenant promises of Christ. Many human contracts contain an escape clause that, under certain circumstances, allows one party or the other to pull out from the agreement; but our God has an everlasting covenant with his people. He will not let us finally fall back and he will under no circumstances draw back himself.

Whether we feel the pressure of our sin or circumstances crushing our Christian faith, or whether in the weakening of our mind in old age we lose hold of all that we once believed, then listen—can you not hear, above the howling hurricane of Satan's fury or the failing frailty of your faith, another calm and clear voice winging its way down the corridors of time to the hearts of his people everywhere: 'I give them eternal life, and they shall never perish; no one will snatch them out of my hand. My Father, who has given them to me, is greater than all; no one can snatch them out of my Father's hand. I and the Father are one' (John 10:28–30)?

In the terror of an awful nightmare, a child wants only the voice of its parents to steady the racing heart, cool the fevered head and clear the tearful eyes. Centuries later, in the lands of exile, the true Israelite had only to turn back to these verses in Leviticus to hear the voice of the covenant God: 'I will remember my covenant … I will not reject them … I am the LORD their God.'

'I am convinced that neither death nor life, neither angels nor demons, neither the present nor the future, nor any powers, neither height nor depth, nor anything else in all creation, will be able to separate us from the love of God that is in Christ Jesus our Lord.'
(Romans 8:38–39)

Day 89 Leviticus 27:1–13
A thankful heart

This final chapter sets out those things that can be pledged to God: humans, animals, property. It may at first appear strange that this should intrude at the end of the book. How much better if Leviticus had ended on the triumphant note of God's promise never to forsake his covenant. However, these 'special vows' are an expression of thankfulness and love or an earnest plea for something. It is as if God was saying: 'I will never break my covenant, but I don't want your obedience to my instructions as a miserable burden; I want a willing and thankful spirit.' These pledges are voluntary—no one is obliged to give. But if we promise God something we must be sure to keep our promise:

'If you make a vow to the LORD your God, do not be slow to pay it, for the LORD your God will certainly demand it of you and you will be guilty of sin. But if you refrain from making a vow, you will not be guilty. Whatever your lips utter you must be sure to do, because you made your vow freely to the LORD your God with your own mouth' (Deuteronomy 23:21–23).

The Israelite is encouraged to make promises to God which they will seal with the pledge of a prized possession. It may be with a member of their own family or with an animal from the heard or flock. In either case, the person or animal need not be given but could be redeemed at a fixed price and the money given to the tabernacle service instead. Here then is an expression of a full heart of gratitude. The measure of gratitude would be the value of the item promised. The priest would value the gift and, where appropriate, what was promised was either given for the service of the tabernacle or the redemption price would be paid. This is how we should understand the vows of Jephthah in Judges 11:30–38 and Hannah in 1 Samuel 1:11. The differing values of men and women and ages is not a measure of significance but of economic worth.

The legend is told of the man who discovered the barn in which Satan stored the seeds he sows in the hearts and minds of men. Noticing that the seeds of discouragement greatly outnumbered the rest, he remarked on this to Satan who replied that they were the easiest seeds to germinate almost anywhere. 'But', he lamented, 'there is one place they will never grow.' 'And where is that?' questioned the man. To which Satan replied, 'In the heart of a grateful man.'

God himself lamented 'You did not serve the LORD your God joyfully and gladly in the time of prosperity' (Deuteronomy 28:47). Can that be said of his people today who live in relative ease in the freedom and comfort of Western society? What is the evidence of my thankful heart to God? What is my greatest treasure to pledge to my Creator Redeemer?

'Let them give thanks to the LORD for his unfailing love and his wonderful deeds for mankind.'

(Psalm 107:8)

Day 90   Leviticus 27:14–25
Our house and home

As people, so property. The Jew might dedicate his house or lands for a particular occasion, but the Christian should be satisfied with something far more. Our property in general and our house in particular ought to be 'holy to the LORD'. And if our house, then our home also. The house is the building, but the home is the warmth of the people. Some Christians live in castles with an efficient portcullis to exclude the visitor and a large moat to drown anyone who dares. First among the property listed by God is the house. Give that to God and the rest should follow. Christians who entertain hospitably and joyfully are normally very willing to lend the rest of their property also. And the reverse is true.

Do your house and home belong to the Lord? A test is this: Who last came to stay, even just for a day or a meal? It used to be commonplace to find this notice displayed in Christian homes:

'Christ is the head of this home.
The silent listener to every conversation.
The unseen guest at every meal.'

But is it true? Should the plaque be kept in the kitchen or thrown into the attic? Many lonely Christians are longing for friendship, but they will never find it only in a church entrance lobby; others need spiritual counsel that can only be given at the fireside or family table. Peter urged on his Christian readers: 'Offer hospitality to one another without grumbling. Each of you should use whatever gift you have received to serve others, as faithful stewards of God's grace in its various forms' (1 Peter 4:9–10).

We may argue that our home is the one place we can relax, where we can escape from the business of life; it is the one thing we can call our own. Exactly. That is why it must be one of the first possessions to devote to the Lord. If we begin by entertaining Christians, we will find what a blessing they can be. But real hospitality is welcoming the stranger into our home. The more of our possessions we devote to God, the richer we become.

However, never forget that God himself is our greatest gift. William Cowper's poem *The Task* was composed in 1784 and contains these lines:

'But, O Thou bounteous Giver of all good!
Thou art of all Thy gifts Thyself the crown;
give what Thou canst, without Thee we are poor;
and with Thee rich, take what Thou wilt away.'

When we stop to consider, we make countless promises in our songs and hymns and prayers. Perhaps we should sing and pray more cautiously.

'When you make a vow to God, do not delay to fulfil it. He has no pleasure in fools; fulfil your vow. It is better not to make a vow than to make one and not fulfil it. Do not let your mouth lead you into sin.'

(Ecclesiastes 5:4–6)

Day 91 Leviticus 27:26–34
Glad obedience

Whilst a vow was a voluntary promise, anything 'devoted to the LORD' was a compulsory offering. Three things are stipulated here: the firstborn of the flock or herd, the man under a divine death penalty, and the tithe in income or harvest. A strange mixture? Perhaps, but not too strange for God to set down before his people. The firstborn represented that which is the best that a man can give, the devoted criminal (v. 29 is not the same as v. 1) or city represented the very worst that a man must avoid (Achan as an individual and Jericho as a city are examples), and the tithe represented the regular portion of income. None of these could be offered as a voluntary pledge because each was an obligation to give.

It is not legitimate for the Christian to offer God as a freewill offering that which it is their plain duty to give; neither should they consider that in shunning some particular evil they have displayed their love commendably to God. For that was no more than their obligation. The regular giving of a portion of our income to the work of the gospel, whether a tenth or more, is no act of charity and good will; it is our spiritual obligation: 'On the first day of every week, each one of you should set aside a sum of money in keeping with your income...' (1 Corinthians 16:1–2).

'These are the commands the LORD gave Moses at Mount Sinai for the Israelites' (v. 34). In this way the book of Leviticus closes. But it did not begin there. It began at the door of the tabernacle, for there is grace. But grace must blossom into obedience. There is a plant sometimes grown in our gardens which has small pink or purple flowers all the way up the stem. It is called *Physostegia virginiana*, better known as 'Obedient plant' because the flowers will stay in whatever position they are turned. The name of all God's people should be similar for the same reason. As the skilled hand of the florist will turn the flowers to display them for their best advantage, so our Lord will, by his word and his Spirit turn us into the best path, always. Ours is only to obey. Willing and happy obedience is one of the most attractive blooms any Christian can display.

The book that opened at the altar, closed on Sinai. Forgiveness expects faithfulness in return; love draws out obedience. Jesus came to make obedient disciples.

'Thanks be to God that, though you used to be slaves to sin, you have come to obey from your heart the pattern of teaching that has now claimed your allegiance. You have been set free from sin and have become slaves to righteousness.'

(Romans 6:17–18)